Twayne's English Authors Series

EDITOR OF THIS VOLUME

Kinley Roby

Northeastern University

G. D. H. Cole

TEAS 255

photograph courtesy of Dame Margaret Cole

G. D. H. Cole

G. D. H. COLE

By GERALD L. HOUSEMAN

Indiana University at Fort Wayne

TWAYNE PUBLISHERS
A DIVISION OF G. K. HALL & CO., BOSTON

Published in 1979 by Twayne Publishers,
A Division of G. K. Hall & Co.
All Rights Reserved

Printed on permanent/durable acid-free paper and bound in the
United States of America

First Printing

Library of Congress Cataloging in Publication Data

Houseman, Gerald L
GDH Cole.

(Twayne's English authors series ; TEAS 255)
Bibliography: p. 144–47
Includes index.
1.   Cole, George Douglas Howard, 1889–1959.
2.   Guild socialism.
HD8393.C57H68   1979   330'.092'4   [B]   78-21665
ISBN 0-8057-6746-0

Contents

About the Author

Gerald L. Houseman is Associate Professor of Political Science at Indiana University — Fort Wayne. He received his B.A. and M.A. degrees at California State University — Hayward and his Ph.D. at the University of Illinois. Born in Iowa and living for fifteen years in California, Professor Houseman wrote his doctoral dissertation on the Australian Labor party and trade union leaders. He has had two extended visits to England in recent years, one in 1973, when he carried out research for this book at Oxford University, and one in the 1975–1976 acadamic year, teaching at New College, Durham, and Newcastle-Upon-Tyne Polytechnic. He has also taught at Brock University, St. Catharines, Ontario, Canada. A recipient of various National Science Foundation, Ford Foundation, National Endowment for the Humanities, and Indiana University grants, Professor Houseman has studied and written about British politics, the British Constitution, Scottish nationalism, the British Labour party, and American urban government, law, and public policy. His study of American law, *The Right of Mobility*, will appear in 1979. His articles and reviews have appeared in *Society, Intellect, A New Political Science, Western Political Quarterly, Canadian Studies in Nationalism*, and the *Proceedings of the Indiana Academy of Social Science*. He has served on the Board of Directors of the Fort Wayne Public Transportation Corporation and of the Caucus for a New Political Science and is National Chairperson of the Committee for Zero Automobile Growth.

Preface

Obscurity has never been a threat to G. D. H. Cole. His prodigious outpouring of books and articles may alone seem to ensure this, but more importantly, the substantive innovation and unique creativity he brought to social literature and to the history of social and political thought have guaranteed his presence in the future.

There was room for doubting this at the time of his death in 1959. There could be no doubt of Cole's immense intellectual and literary contributions to British and Western Socialism, but it was difficult for very many to see Socialist traditions continuing to exist in any meaningful form. The movement in the West which generally has been described as Democratic Socialism appeared to have a small place in the future scheme of things.

The 1950s were bad years for Socialism in Britain. The accomplishments of the 1945–51 Labour government were generally acknowledged, but were viewed through the prisms of cynicism and despair which inevitably accompany the loss of empire and economic position in the world. The attitude which became popularized as "I'm All Right, Jack" was clearly in evidence and indeed prevalent. The political apathy and melancholia of John Osborne's play *The Angry Young Man* symbolized the feelings of post-Suez Britain as it languished under the ineptitude of its political leadership. The few strands of political ideology which had been important to pragmatic Britain did not bear up well in this decade of crisis.

In the United States these were the Eisenhower years, a decade of apathy, conformity, and postwar suburban boom. More importantly, these were the Joe McCarthy years, when an attachment to Democratic Socialism, to say nothing of Socialism in other forms, gave birth to suspicion. It was true, of course, that Britain and even the United States had carried out some Socialist experimentation, but it was by this time too commonly suspected that such schemes as the British national health service most probably had derived their impetus from Moscow.

In the mid-1970s, G. D. H. Cole has reemerged. He is the subject of new books, articles, monographs, and dissertations. His works are being reprinted in bright new formats, class papers and guest seminars are devoted to him, and organizations which, in his time, he might have led or had a hand in, are forming and growing. People for Self-Management, for example, is a remarkably large United States group which is devoted to the study of workers' control schemes, something close to Cole's heart, but also to the development of community frameworks in which people decide those matters which are important to them rather than having decisions made for them by bureaucrats. This latter goal was of paramount importance to Cole. The Canadians and the British have set up institutes for the study of workers' control of industry, worker consultation has become a part of the British Government's "social contract" policy, and such schemes have recently worked their way into Australian Labor party platforms.

What accounts for this reemergence? In the most succinct terms, Cole can be said to represent the two most important impulses of the New Left of the 1960s and 1970s: a belief in Socialist values, including equality and humanity, coupled with a belief in small government. Cole could not abide sprawling bureaucracies, for he felt that they were inimical to, indeed the antithesis of, Democratic Socialism. Cole's political and social outlook can therefore serve as a central reference point for the New Left and its activists and, perhaps more importantly, for anyone interested in rediscovering and studying the combination of Socialism and small government.

If such a combination appears to be paradoxical, consider these: Cole was an antimonarchist with an aristocratic demeanor, an atheist who believed in Socialism because of its "spirit," a revolutionary who sought to implement his ideas through conventional means, a democrat who did not believe in Parliament, a friend of many Americans who strongly disliked the United States, and a middle–class professional who identified his own personal needs with those of the working class. It will be shown, however, that there are really no paradoxes at work here at all. Instead, there are explanations for these outlooks as well as for this most important point: individualism and Socialism are complementary. Certainly the ideas of Socialism imply the presence of collective decision-making in approaching economic or political questions and collective action in obtaining results. G. D. H. Cole believed nonetheless that individuality of expression, creativity, a sense of aesthetics, and development of character relied upon a social setting in which the entrepreneurial spirit—what he sometimes called the "spirit of grab"—was absent, as well as upon a cooperative atmosphere in which opportunity for an individual sense of fulfillment was not only present but pervasive. He was not dogmatic about this. His mind was always open to the possibilities of change, and he proceeded to Socialism from an aesthetic perspective as much as from a moral perspective.

One of the goals of this study is to find and examine the reasons for the revived interest in Cole as a major figure in twentieth-century English political literature and philosophy. Achieving this requires delving into his thought, especially his original contributions and formulations, and this in turn requires a brief review of his life and of the environment in which he lived and worked. Generalizations will be developed and applied as these tasks are undertaken, but a full understanding of Cole also requires analysis of his major works and of some representative works. A great deal of selectivity and discrimination must of course be applied to his prodigious output. His most important social science and historical works will therefore be emphasized, to some degree at the expense of his pamphlets and articles, which were generally devoted to rather transitory or current concerns; and some of his ephemeral efforts, such as his detective novels, will be ignored altogether. Between these general and specific perspectives on Cole, it is hoped, the outline of his intellect and character can be discerned and appreciated and the relevance and foresight of his innovative mind can be realized.

A number of acknowledgments are in order. Dame Margaret Cole granted me a most useful interview at her home in Ealing, and also did an intensive critique of the first draft. The staff of Nuffield College Library, Oxford, especially Eva Nelson, was helpful to me in making use of the Cole Collection. Anthony Wright of the University College of North Wales at Bangor was studying the Cole Collection at the same time and he, along with several others, made helpful suggestions or contributed some very useful ideas. My secretary, Barbara Blauvelt, has been most helpful. Finally, my wife, Penny, and my children, Kit, Lisa, and

Vicki, have all helped in their individual ways and have provided inspiration.

GERALD L. HOUSEMAN

Fort Wayne, Indiana

Chronology

1889   Born at Cambridge, England, on September 25, the youngest of three children; soon afterwards the family moved to Ealing, a London suburb.

1902–   Attended St. Paul's School, Hammersmith.
1908

1908–   Attended Balliol College, Oxford.
1912

1908   Joined Oxford Fabian Society and Ealing Branch of the Independent Labour party.

1909–   Founder and Editor of *Oxford Reformer*.
1911

1912   Balliol degree in "Greats" with first class honors.

1912   Lecturer at Armstrong College, Newcastle-on-Tyne.

1912–   Prize Fellow of Magdalen College, Oxford.
1919

1913   Published first major work, *The World of Labour*.

1914   Joined Fabian Research Committee, later the Fabian Research Department; elected to Fabian Society Executive Committee.

1915   Resigned from Fabian Society; Honorary Secretary, Fabian Research Department. One of the founders of the National Guilds League

1917   Published *Self-Government in Industry*.

1918   Married Margaret Postgate; began to publish articles in the *New Statesman*.

1920   Published *Guild Socialism Restated*.

1920   Labor correspondent of the *Manchester Guardian*.

1921   Director of tutorial classes, University of London.

1923   Decline and collapse of the National Guilds League.

1925   Reader in Economics and Fellow of University College, Oxford.

1926   Strong effort in support of the General Strike.

1928   Rejoined the Fabian Society.

1929 Returned to London.
1930 Labour candidate for Parliament for King's Norton, Birmingham; foundation of Society for Socialist Inquiry and Propaganda.
1931 Founded the New Fabian Research Bureau.
1935 Moved to Hendon, a North London suburb.
1939 New Fabian Research Bureau joined with the Fabian Society; Cole served as chairman of the society from 1939–1946 and 1948–1950.
1941–Director, Nuffield Reconstruction Survey.
1944
1944 Professor and Fellow of All Souls College, Oxford.
1945 Parliamentary candidate for university seat.
1949 Initiates conferences aimed at production of *New Fabian Essays*.
1951 Chairman and Director of UNESCO Seminar on Workers Education.
1953 Publication of first of Cole's multi-volume *History of Socialist Thought*.
1956 President of International Society for Socialist Studies.
1957 Chairman of the Board, New Statesman Publishing Company; moved to inner London (Kensington); Honorary Fellow of Balliol College, Oxford, and Research Fellow of Nuffield College, Oxford, upon retirement as Professor and Fellow of All Souls College, Oxford.
1958 Visiting Fellow, Roosevelt University, Chicago.
1959 Death on January 14.

CHAPTER 1

The Social and Political Environment in which Cole Studied and Worked

G. D. H. Cole's life spanned a period of British industrial growth, maturity, and decline, the development of the United States and the Soviet Union into major world powers, two world wars, a great deal of progress and innovation in such fields as transportation, commerce, and communications, the growth of consumer services, and several boom-and-bust cycles of the modern capitalism which he so thoroughly opposed and detested. Cole also witnessed the rise and fall of Fascist regimes on the Continent and the perilous threat to Britain's continued existence which developed in the early years of World War II. He saw the success of a Socialist revolution in Russia, the questioning of that success, and the often disappointing leadership and policymaking of Democratic Socialist governments and movements in Western Europe.

Europe and the world were generally in one state of crisis or another during the whole of his lifetime, and Cole surely, as much as the next person, had difficulty in grasping and coping with these events. His education, life-style, codes, habits, and personality reflected a softness and humanity of a far less cataclysmic age, a gentility born of detailed study of great writers and thinkers, of Oxford ambience, and of a concern for aesthetics which found its way not only into an interest in literature and art, but into such concerns as the design of buildings and cities as well as of politics and society; in short, of an aesthetic view of life.

A walk through the Cotswold Hills, Cole's favorite walking place, or down the "High" or Broad Street in Oxford, or perhaps even through the London suburb of Ealing can still be informative and a worthwhile venture for anyone who seeks to understand Cole's environment. It is even possible that Cole was subconsciously thinking of Oxford and the small communities of its separate colleges when he posited the advantages of decision-making by small groups, the disadvantages of centralization and bureacracy, and the need for representative systems to be based upon function rather than upon geographic proximity or mere numbers.[1] His entire life was spent in one of two places, London or Oxford. He did not travel a great deal because of health reasons, and he largely confined himself to Western Europe. His only visit to America, for example, took place just one year before he died; and although there is certainly no hard proof, it is reasonable to assume some connection between this fact and his "Little Englander" outlook, which was so important until World War II.

The lifetime of Cole also coincides with the rise of the Left as a significant factor in British politics. Socialist ideology, in part because of the efforts of the Fabian Society, seeped into the consciousness of many British workers and intellectuals and took root in the sharp class divisions which have characterized British society since well before the Industrial Age. The Labour party surpassed Liberal strength in the 1920s and replaced that party as the alternative to the Tories. The trade-union movement grew to maturity and assumed an intensely bureaucratic form. Various other Socialist and Leftist organizations also came into prominence, including the cooperative movement, workers' education groups, and womens' Socialist auxiliaries.

The comfortable days and ways of Edwardian England have been popular topics of both fiction and nonfiction despite all that is known about the inequality, repression, and want which existed at that time. The Webbs and their work on the Poor Laws commend themselves to anyone misled by some of the fictions about this period or by the carefree Disney movies which are often set in this period even when the work upon which they are based was originally set in some other time. This time, in which G. D. H. Cole was growing up, was no more immune to the injustices of the world than any other. The Boer War established grim and foreboding truths about the world in much the same way as the Spanish Civil War would in the 1930s, with the weaponry and triumph of Fascism analogous to the British innovation of the concentration camp at the turn of the century in South Africa.

British imperialism was in full flower, and the aura of Kiplingesque verse and story conveniently foreclosed, for the unthinking and the unaware, the possibility that it might all be wrong. Things did appear, after all, to be going well for the British middle class, whatever the lot of the poor might have been or whatever the world might have thought. In this age of economic growth and near-miraculous technological innovation and progress, it was difficult to be pessimistic and even more difficult to be a rebellious social critic.

But for Cole it was natural. Nothing in the writings of William Morris, his political, social, ideological, spiritual, aesthetic, and moralistic mentor, suggested any equation of technology and progress. Morris had said that there would have to be more machinery before there could be less, but this was not a sign of progress; it meant that things would have to get worse before they could get better.[2] This was quite a different outlook from that of the orthodox Marxian Socialists, who believed that the problem was not one of technology but of who controlled it and who reaped its benefits. In this sense the tradition of which Cole is a part—a tradition which includes Morris and the Medievalist Movement as well as John Ruskin,[3] and which in recent years includes such disparate and important thinkers as Lewis Mumford, Jacques Ellul, Herbert Marcuse, Hannah Arendt, Paul Goodman, and Theodore Roszak—can be considered much more radical than that of the orthodox Marxists. The definition of a radical referred to is the more traditional one which characterizes those who seek out the root of a problem.

Cole's individualism and intellectuality precluded any dogmatic attachment to institutions or organizations of any kind, but the urgent necessity for encouraging and promoting political action of certain types required his association with a variety of groups and causes and even, on occasion, with government. His most important associations were with the Fabian Society, the British trade-union movement, and the political instrument of which both were a part, the British Labour party. In each case, Cole experienced difficulty in accepting the terms, conditions, and above all, the discipline, of membership and association. He realized the commonality of goals which made it necessary to work with each of these groups, but a tension always existed in these relationships, a tension not unlike that which he experienced in defining his relationship to British society. Cole was nearly always in a minority position on most important political and social issues, and though he was occasionally frustrated, he usually adjusted well to this fact and assumed a philosophical stance.[4]

It was natural that Cole would be attracted to the Fabian Society.[5] It was, firstly, a Socialist society. It also was a collection of formidable intellectuals who were not content with a debating society or mere social outlet, but were people who used the society as a base for lecturing, pamphleteering, and frank agitation for Socialism. This was not done through dogmatic or emotional harangues. Fabians sought out the facts, believing that the facts would generally be with them, that statistics, policy studies, and aggregate data would almost by themselves stress the need for transformation to a Socialist Britain. It is an understatement to say that the Fabians were research-oriented. Sidney and Beatrice Webb had set the tone for the society from about 1890 (it was founded in 1884), carrying out and promoting hard-headed research efforts which had received the acclaim of social reformers, Socialists, and intellectuals alike.[6] The society attracted a collection of some of the best minds in Britain, including George Bernard Shaw, Graham Wallas, Sydney Olivier, and, for a time, H. G. Wells. The guiding stars, all the same, were the Webbs, who promoted trade unionism, developing models of action and organization, sought reform of local government, agitated for social welfare measures, studied and sought change of the Poor Laws, and developed cooperative, municipal and state ownership alternatives to capitalism. The Fabians were also instrumental in the founding of the Labour party in 1900, and the society has always been formally linked to the party as a small but influential federated group.

The Webbs had a marked influence upon Cole, but not in the way one might suppose.[7] The society never set down in specific terms just what kind of Socialism it favored, limiting itself to its very general statement known as "The Basis," and this was one of the reasons Cole could feel comfortable in it. At the time Cole joined the society, the mainstream of Fabianism was nevertheless a Webbian collectivist outlook. Cole never shared this view, and none of the descriptions he has written of Socialism reveal anything like the Webbs' devout insistence upon state ownership of industry and services nor the enthusiasm they displayed later in their lives over the Soviet experiment. Cole specifically repudiated such models of politics, government, and society, and his ideals are most assuredly not found in the all-powerful state and its bureaucratic control over the lives of people. His life was devoted to a steadfast but ever-broadening belief in Guild Socialism, and the ramifications of this unique view, as set out in his writings, is the principal concern of this study.

The Webbs therefore did not influence Cole through their political and social theories, but rather in the tradition they set of meticulous research, of the gathering of facts and statistics, and of the employment of these in marshaling Socialist arguments of significant force. Cole made use of this tradition in laying waste to some of the Webbs' assumptions just as he did in leveling well-placed blows against the apologias of *status quo* advocates. There were also great differences in temperament between the Webbs and Cole, some of which are merely explained by personality differences and others which are probably due to differences in background. Sidney Webb had been a civil servant, and the approaches which he and Beatrice took to problems and issues were considered more pragmatic and perhaps less academic than was generally the case with Cole.[8]

Cole resigned from the Fabian Society in 1915 in what has now become a well-publicized set of differences with the Webbs and others. He did not return to the society until 1928, and after the society had stagnated and nearly passed out of existence, it was Cole who revived it and who recreated a relevant role for it in Socialist and Labour affairs.

Cole's reexamination of his role in Fabianism in the late 1920's was matched with a reexamination of his position vis-à-vis the Labour party, another organization with which he always had a love-hate relationship. His first preference had always been the Independent Labour party, which was historically more militant than Labour and which had the virtue of being a Socialist party, in fact if not in name, from the time of its founding in the early 1880s under Keir Hardie. Hardie, the first working–class member of Parliament and a man of great character and persuasion, was to Cole's mind a hero.[9] The future, for a variety of reasons, appeared to lay with Labour in the late 1920s and Cole, unhappy as he was with some of its principles and its *modus operandi*, to say nothing of some of its leaders, was willing to work within it and for it for the rest of his life.

. . . dissatisfied as I am with much in the Labour Party, I remain in it and adjure my fellow Socialists to play an active part in its work. I do this, because there is no alternative to it that holds out any promise of becoming the political instrument of a mass-drive towards Socialism, and because I do not want to waste my energies in splinter movements that have no stability or prospect of durable success. The Labour Party, with all its shortcomings, is the party of the working class . . . there is clearly for the present nothing in the least competent to take its place. In the last resort, my loyalty is not owing to the Labour Party, or to any political party, but to Socialism, of which no political party can be more than a necessary instrument. But within this greater loyalty, I owe a loyalty to the Labour Party as the party of the workers, which I must do all I can to make more fully Socialist. . . .[10]

He was Labour's candidate for a Birmingham seat in 1930 and for a university seat (a seat which does not exist today) in 1945. His great importance to the Labour party, however, can be found in a tremendous amount of writing and research he carried out for it. Some of his pamphlets, books, and other writings are still published and sold by the party.

His relationship with Labour was nevertheless tense and strained. He was not overly enthusiastic about the programs and achievements of the 1945–51 Labour government, although he supported some of these (steel nationalization is a notable example), and he was severely critical of the terms of the American loan which the Labour government contracted for; but the severity of this and other criticisms of postwar Labour pales beside his statements and writings on the two Ramsay MacDonald Labour governments, particularly the second, which held power during the Great Depression. MacDonald's successful move to cut social welfare in 1931 was not only bad economics, as both Cole and the general theses of even capitalist Keynesian economics could easily show, but was inhumane to the working class.[11]

The British trade–union movement was another of Cole's great concerns. It may be difficult to understand and to assess some of his attitudes toward the trade unions unless it is realized that the British trade unions are, for the most part, considerably older than those of the United States. Union agitation and strikes took place at the turn of the nineteenth century in both countries, but the subsequent growth and earlier acceptance of trade unions in Britain, despite violent resistance, judicial findings of conspiracy, transportation to Australia, and brutal suppression made the trade unions a significant economic factor at a much earlier point in time. Certainly they were a major factor by the time Cole was attending Oxford.

It is also important to point out that trade unions are organized somewhat differently in Britain than in the United States. Most American unions represent the workers in a given plant, shop, office, or store, which is a bargaining unit established (since 1935) by election of the employees. British unions are of course evident in factories, offices, and shops, and in fact are more highly organized, more pervasive, and represent a much larger share of the organizable employees than is the case in the United States. But they are organized on a branch basis rather than on a bargaining-unit basis. They are organized along geographic lines, and the union branch, or "local union," as it would be called in America, represents employees of a number of firms of the same type or of the same trade in a given locale. The engineering workers of Peterborough or the dock workers of Liverpool are examples.

Cole's Guild Socialist outlook emphasized self-government of each department or division of a particular factory or shop; thus Cole's position was at odds with the traditional organizational forms of trade unions in Britain. He believed the unions to be far too bureaucratic, and he did not believe that unions should be organized along branch or trade lines. What is far more important, however, is the fact that the unions, in his view, did not accede to a democratic structure, and for this reason he was often distrustful of union officials and stated that he would not like to see them come into control of the guilds which he thought should be organized in conformity with his Guild Socialist framework.[12] He was also highly critical of the structure of the Annual Conference of the Labour party, which is supposedly the supreme authority on party policymaking, because it sets up an unfair scheme of representation in which union leaders can cast up to several million votes for the candidates or policies of their choice.[13]

Cole usually found British trade unions to be unimaginative, incredibly dull, stratified of structure to a most complex degree, and badly led. He also somewhat grudgingly recognized that the

unions undeniably did speak to the interests and welfare of their
members, and for this reason he worked with them in economic
research, workers' education, and political activities in which
both Cole and the unions maintained an interest. He was
particularly fond of the class-conscious workers he met in the
Workers Educational Association and in the Independent Labour
Party.[14] As with the Fabian Society and the Labour party, his
support of the trade-union movement was rooted as much in
praxis as in theory. He supported the trade unions because they
were, in word and deed, a working-class movement, but his
attitude was nonetheless tempered with a strong and nagging
dissatisfaction.

Beyond the Fabians, the Labour party, and the unions, Cole
had several organizational and institutional attachments. Some of
them, such as Oxford University, were very important, and the
National Guilds League, which will be discussed further, is of
obvious importance since it embraced Cole's ideals of the good
society. Some groups, such as the Independent Labour party and
his experimental Society for Socialist Inquiry and Propaganda,
faltered upon ideological or personality differences.[15] The
Cooperative movement is a good example of a cause which was
always close to Cole's heart, although again there is clear
evidence of impatience and disappointment.[16] In the later years
of his life, Cole headed an International Society for Socialist
Studies, which reflected both his rather late-found internationalism and his disappointment with the Labour party and its
domestic performance, but which also reflected his consistent
opposition to any Socialism built upon Leviathan principles.[17]

Cole was by no measure an organization man, and his
relationships with the various and sundry groups which were
important to him were always characterized by a set of qualifiers
wrought by his consistent idealism. This does not mean that he
did not work hard and well for these groups; on the contrary, he
was extremely valuable to all of them. It only means that, to
Cole, the ideals were of paramount importance. He was an
idealist to the last, just as he had been from the beginning of his
life and from his first reading of William Morris.

CHAPTER 2

Life and Careers

I became a Socialist more than fifty years ago when I read *News from Nowhere* as a schoolboy and realised quite suddenly that William Morris had shown me the vision of a society in which it would be a fine and fortunate experience to live. Needless to say, I have not lived in such a society, or in any even remotely like it; but I cound myself not the less fortunate to have been shown that vision; and I can truthfully say that from the day when I first read *News from Nowhere* my socialist convictions have remained firmly fixed.
—G. D. H. Cole, *William Morris as a Socialist*[1]

EVEN before going to Oxford in 1908, G. D. H. Cole was a committed Socialist. More than that, he was already well into the particular mold of Socialist that he would always be, an aesthetic and nondogmatic type who would not be particularly offended if one did not agree with him. What did offend him was social and economic injustice, and he always was willing to fight injustice with any of the worthy tools he could muster, whether it was a withering argument, an abrasive wit, or a well-chosen bit of prose.

These were not merely weapons to be unleashed at a particularly propitious point in a debate, however. They were a part of a personality that was much more warm than such a description would indicate. Perhaps he did not seem warm at first to those who were introduced to him through his lectures, which were crisp, formalistic, highly informative, and delivered with the style of an aristocrat. To those who came to know him on a less formal basis, his fellow Socialists, academic colleagues, or members of the "Cole group," a nonexclusive group of Oxford students who were especially interested in developing their

21

consciousness of public affairs, the warmth, the wit, and indeed the charm of Professor Cole were familiar. Kingsley Martin, the *New Statesman* editor and writer, went so far as to describe him as a "secular saint," a man of very strong convictions who was more than willing to fight for them but who never insisted that one need accept a bit of his outlook.[2]

This great devotion to Cole was not limited to the "Cole group" or to his immediate circle of friends, for his prolific writings became well known beyond the shores of Britain and have recently developed a fresh, new devotion evidenced by the fact that he is "in vogue" among a certain number of scholars in history, literature, and the social sciences. To many individuals, those to whom ideals are important, Cole represents the best of two worlds—Socialism, a system of economic democracy, combined with small government organized in such a way that most important decision-making is carried out at the small group level—in short, a system of political democracy with a high degree of accountability. This attractive combination obtains an even higher place in the firmament when it has been set out by a person of consummate skills, brilliant mind, and high purpose, whose devotion to principle, gentleness of disposition, love of beauty, and articulate exposition of the cause of humanity characterized his entire life. It is little wonder that he was considered a man of vision, a guru to his generations, a "secular saint." A.J.P. Taylor, who subscribed to all of this, summed it up: ". . . Cole came as near to complete integrity as any man of his time. I venerated him."[3]

I *The Early Years: Cole's Careers and Achievements*

George Douglas Howard Cole was born on September 25, 1889, in Cambridge, England. His parents shortly thereafter moved to the London suburb of Ealing, where he was raised, where he also lived later in his life, and where his widow, Dame Margaret Cole, lives today. He was the youngest of three children, having two elder sisters, and of his three names, it was Douglas that was used most, though many friends simply used his first three initials.[4] He apparently had a rather ordinary middle–class upbringing, attending St. Paul's school in Hammersmith before going to Balliol, one of the most distinguished colleges at Oxford. He succeeded exceptionally well at Oxford, for he was awarded a Prize Fellowship of seven years' duration at Magdalen College, Oxford, which required no teaching duties and gave him an apartment next to the College's famous Deer Park. Deer are still kept, incidentally, at the College today, and the surroundings of Magdalen and Oxford generally are much as they were then. The fellowship launched his academic and writing career, although he had already done some writing and publishing at Balliol as editor of the *Oxford Reformer*.[5] The brilliance of the student Cole was not limited to his writing of papers and examinations. One of his contemporaries, Ivor Brown, has remembered that

any company which he entered seemed quickened by his coming and that any group to which he spoke felt a rise in the intellectual temperature. But he could be most icy if he chose and he chose to be so in Chapel. Attendance on Sundays was then compulsory, and Cole, like many others of us, appearing under protest and taking no part in the proceedings, was magiificent in his aloofness and formidable in his non-participation.[6]

The chief memories of Cole as a student are not in this vein, however, and his warmth, good humor, erudition, and conviction are those elements of his character that remain strongest in the minds of those who knew him then.[7]

He married Margaret Postgate in 1918, and she was not only his wife, but his coauthor, coactivist in politics, and intellectual partner. Dame Margaret Cole's contributions to political and social litarature are very great, for she not only coauthored a large number of books with Cole, but is the author herself of well over thirty books. She is probably best known as editor of the diaries of Beatrice Webb and as author of *The Story of Fabian Socialism, Growing Up Into Revolution*, and *The Life of G. D. H. Cole*.[8] She must by any account be considered a social historian of significance, and she is prolific, for her articles in papers and journals such as the *New Statesman, Tribune, Political Quarterly, The Observer*, and the London *Times* number in the hundreds if not in the thousands. She has also written a number of Fabian pamphlets as well as a great many items which do not bear her name. She writes a monthly column for *Socialist Commentary*, the Fabianish journal which concentrates on foreign affairs. None of the above includes the more than thirty detective stories which she and Douglas Cole wrote in their "spare time." Margaret also had a great deal to do with the Fabian Society, serving as its secretary, and with the workers' education movement as well as a variety of Socialist and Leftist causes. She met Cole when she was a young Cambridge graduate and researcher in the Labour Research Department.[9]

The marriage, to all appearances, was a joining of very like-minded and yet independent equals. At certain junctures in their life it was necessary for one to work in London while the other was at Oxford, but this did not signify any lack of compatibility or affection. It merely demonstrated an exigency of their busy lives and duties. Her intelligence and judgment were always respected by her husband, though none of this intruded upon their mutual sense of humor and their engaging use of wit, occasionally at the expense of one another. She was also a steadfast companion and helpmate, and this was made particularly noticeable by his perennial health problems.[10]

One of Cole's most important roles in life was that of educator. This is true in the formal sense of that term, for he taught at various Oxford colleges and in London, but it is also true in the broader sense. He was always an intellectual, and he approached issues, problems, and conceptualizations with a precise, clear, and logical frame of mind. He made use of such processes' as dialectical thinking, and he enjoyed the stimulation of dialogue, debate, and discussion.[11]

He was particularly keen on workers' education, and he was therefore helpful to the Workers Educational Association, to trade union and Labour party efforts of this kind, and to Ruskin College, Oxford, which is devoted to workers' education and to studies which are felt to be of concern to workers and the working class. Cole's most innovative work as a teacher was probably in the field of workers' education. He is considered one of the pioneers in this effort, and it was important to him both as a Socialist and as an educator. Workers' education had a difficult time gaining acceptance because it carried an implication, from the very beginning, of support for trade unionism and for the workers' cause. This is remarkable in light of the acceptance of business education and business-oriented education which had occurred long before, but it is perhaps not surprising in a capitalist system. Even the field of industrial relations, which only implies acceptance of the existence of unions and not the support of them, has been a fairly late arrival in Western higher education. Cole was strongly interested in industrial relations as well as workers' education—*Self-Government in Industry* can in some ways be considered a textbook on the subject—but his efforts as well as his sympathies were more closely drawn to the latter. Cole placed his faith in the kinds of workers he met in the WEA, and the workers' education movement has today spread to New Zealand, Canada, the United States, and most of the Western world. The acceptance and expansion of this endeavor still has a long way to go in the United States, for example, where only one Ph.D. program in the field is in existence; in Britain, its greater longevity has yielded greater acceptance, and the WEA and Ruskin College manage to thrive, with a good part of the credit for this due to Cole.

Support of trade unionism as one of the premises of workers' education can in no way be construed as an injection of bias by Cole into the professional and ethical principles which served him as an educator. Cole quite openly worried about fulfilling his task as a university teacher while balancing this against his dedication to his political views and especially his Socialist outlook. He believed that this required an "adjustment" which

is bound to be most difficult for the teacher of controversial subjects whose views are unorthodox in that they cut up against the prevailing political and economic system. For he has largely to train people to live in the system and cannot go all out to persuade them to change it. I admit that the distinction between "education" and "propaganda" is in the last resort an illogical distinction, because all education contains some elements of propaganda, though not necessarily in a political sense. No one complains of the teacher of literature for trying to persuade his students to admire Keats. . . . But if a teacher of economics displays too sharply his preference of the second kind as well as of the first, he will speedily be accused of abusing his position in order to further his political views. Nor is this quite unreasonable. For it is his business to teach his pupils Marshall and Hayek as well as Marx and to leave to them the task of making up their own minds which set of doctrines to believe in. Unless he is prepared to take up this attitude, he has no business to be a teacher at the University. . . .[12]

Cole's realization of his position to influence can be especially well taken in the light of the strong impression he made not only upon the minds of fellow Britishers, but upon students who later

made their way back to their homes in the United States,
Canada, India, Australia, Africa, and other places. Cabinet
members and other leaders of governments around the world
have been taught and influenced by Cole, and he is well
remembered by many of his students. The former Deputy Prime
Minister of Australia, Dr. Jim Cairns, writes:

> . . .I attended many of Cole's lectures and seminars. I found him really
> to be quite uninterested in Australia. My other impressions were that he
> was a prolific worker with a prodigious memory, even to the finest
> details, of the Labour movement in the nineteenth century. He was a
> precise and effective lecturer who often spoke from memory with
> correct details in abundance which made it difficult to believe that he
> was not reading prepared material. . . . I found him always to be a
> psychological rebel with an aristocratic nature. . . .[13]

Students of Cole were never given brusque treatment, despite
his aristocratic bent. This did happen, even at Oxford, to those
who worked under others; but Cole was regarded as "a poised
and beautiful spirit" whose conduct of tutorials was carried out
with "such briskness and kindness that one is encouraged to
excellence."[14] There was a certain aloofness even in these
however, and a former student has said that many students liked
him but could not really be close to him. Some former students
recall Cole's Oxford room in which he held his tutoring sessions.
A large gramophone with a grotesquely large bell dominated the
Edwardian atmosphere so that one anonymous recollection is
that "it was really like Professor Higgins' place." His lectures
appeared to be as superhuman as his prodigious and scholarly
writing, and every one of his ideas was pregnant with well-
ordered premises. It was said that he "teaches without techni-
que. . . . His erudition is never paraded in pomp. Surely few
minds in the twentieth century have been tidier or fuller."[15]

Cole's best-known role, of course, is as a writer. Though
considerably greater attention will be given to his literary and
social-science contributions, a summary of their relationship to
this most famous aspect of his career is in order. The many
students of political theory who study Rousseau are often
acquainted with Cole's translation of *The Social Contract and
Discourses* and with Cole's generally helpful and insightful
introduction to this translation.[16] Many of Cole's tracts,

pamphlets, histories, texts, speculations, and contemporary analyses provide period pieces for anyone interested in British social, economic, labor, or political history. Cole's biographies of such men as Robert Owen, John Burns, William Morris, Keir Hardie, and William Cobbett provide original analyses of these figures. His hundreds of columns and commentaries in the *New Statesman* and other journals are of course mirrors of their time but also of Cole's steadfastness of principle and flexibility of approach to social, economic, and political problem-solving. They are also alive with his sharpness of wit, command of language, and warm humanity. His small book on Karl Marx has received some acclaim, and his *magnum opus*, the five-volume *History of Socialist Thought*, filled a great void. Some observers believe that this work and his other well-known histories—of the working class of Britain, of the "common people," of the Labour party, and of the Cooperative movement, to cite four kinds of prominent examples—mark his most significant achievements as those of a social and labor historian.[17]

He could also claim some considerable credit as an economist, though this definition of Cole requires qualification. He cannot be considered to have been conversant with modern methological approaches or with a very proficient use of models or of mathematics, but he made significant contributions as an economic historian and as a dedicated researcher who dug out a great many fugitive facts, statistics, and materials. He was conversant with economic theory and economic theorists, and he has provided some unique interpretations of these.

His most unique and significant contributions, however, are those he made in his role as an original political writer. More than anyone else—and this is generally recognized—he set down, elaborated, and revised Guild Socialist theory so that it played a historic role in British political thought, and, perhaps even more significantly, it appears to have renewed relevance today. This is also the paramount consideration to be examined in any survey of Cole's thought.

A great deal of Cole's eminence, especially in the years immediately following his graduation from Oxford and proceeding through the early 1930s, rested upon a general perception of Cole as a politician. He has been described as a back-room politician, one who sought no glory but instead fought for principle.[18] It is conceivable that one could set this down as

another of the important roles he performed, as long as it is
maintained that Cole cannot be considered a politician within
the context of the usual meaning of that term; but, all things
considered, he should probably not be thought of as a politician
at all. He was concerned with politics, he dabbled in politics as a
candidate and as a propagandist, he wrote about politics, and he
worried about politics. Politics envelops every person in every
society;[19] but to one who is concerned with social questions, with
the elimination of injustice, and with a vision of a better life for
all, it takes on a special pertinence and a particular urgency. Cole
did not therefore eschew politics or avoid political consequences, but his view of politics nevertheless placed some limits
on its importance to him. Politics was viewed as a necessary set of
relationships, plural in character, which could lead to more
politics and more societal relationships of the kind with which
Cole was familiar through most of his lifetime, or it could lead to
greater oppression and inhumanity, or it could lead to something
better than humanity had ever experienced: to an end of
acquisitiveness and exploitation, to William Morris's "Nowhere,"
to Socialism, and to the good society. Cole was therefore active
in politics and in time became a significant political theorist, but
he never was a politician.

    He liked some politicians and he enjoyed their company. He
played an important role in the education and political
socialization of some of them. He also enjoyed debate and
discussion, and this was one of the reasons, it can be assumed,
that he joined the Fabian Society while at Oxford and remained a
Fabian for seven years. He served the society as one of its shining
new lights, and he joined with relish into its activities of
lecturing, writing, propaganda, and pamphleteering. But the
failure of Cole and his group of rebellious young research
associates to take control of the Fabian Society in 1915 resulted
in their resignations and their establishment of the National
Guilds League.

    The immediate issue in the society was the question of
continued affiliation with the Labour party. The party was not
committed to Socialism at this time. Cole, a newly elected
member of the Fabian Executive, proposed withdrawal on these
grounds. The proposal was also motivated by Cole's attitude
toward the trade unions, which were an important bureaucratic
and un-Socialist element in the party, and by his attitude toward

the Webbs, who had been instrumental in the founding of the Labour party in 1900. The vote of disaffiliation went strongly against Cole, who then announced his resignation from the society and who, it is reported, denounced the membership as "bloody fools."[20] He would not return to the society until thirteen years later. The victory over Cole and his rebellious young clique was shortlived, however, for the society soon languished and became moribund.[21] The National Guilds League, on the other hand, was to flourish for a few years under the leadership of Cole and S. G. Hobson.

II   *The Guild Socialist Movement*

Hobson initiated the Guild Socialist movement in 1912 with a series of articles in the *New Age,* a weekly which was of considerable importance to the movement. A. R. Orage, its editor, was one of its leading supporters, although A. J. Penty had published *The restoration of the Gild System* six years before and may technically lay claim to being the originator of the movement. Penty, interestingly enough, had been a disciple of William Morris and had also had some unsatisfying experiences with the Fabian Society. It was, nevertheless, Hobson, Orage, Cole, and the *New Age* who in the beginning gave Guild Socialism its thrust and its influence.[22]

These men were impressed by the antibureaucratic and strongly anarchic strain found in Syndicalist Socialism, which had been imported from France. Although Syndicalist writers were quite unclear about the details of the society and state they envisioned, they sought one in which the least possible state authority would be exercised and in which systems of representation relied upon function, upon the role which one carried out in society, and upon the *syndicat* with which an individual is affiliated. There was no role for capitalists in such a system, and industry and services would be controlled by the workers and not by the state. Syndicalism was influential in Socialist thought in Europe until the success of the Russian Revolution, and it had a marked influence upon the Industrial Workers of the World, the IWW, in the United States. The Big State doctrines of the Webbs and the Fabians, by contrast, were dreary, unimaginative, and far too confident of what might occur under state control of industry.[23] Syndicalism placed heavy emphasis upon the workers' "myth," which was basically a belief in themselves and their destined victory, upon violence, upon a revolutionary cult of cadre forces, and upon a great faith in the ultimate weapon of the General Strike. The "myth" was an apocalyptic and antirational vision in which the inevitable success of revolution was expected to reach achievement through heroic, but also violent and aggressive, acts. The concept of "separateness," as set out by George Sorel, one of Syndicalism's principal writers, was analogous to Lenin's idea of the need for a dedicated hard core of full-time revolutionaries committed to violent overthrow of the state. Such individuals were "separate" from the other strata and elements of society so that they could avoid cooptation by the capitalist elite. The ultimate weapon of the Syndicalists, the General Strike, would presumably be effected at the appropriate time to bring down the state and the capitalist class which it served.[24]

It was hardly the kind of view that Englishmen are wont to take of politics or of life. The sympathy of Cole and the Guild Socialists for Syndicalism therefore hardly ever amounted to more than that, and the doctrine seemed starkly impractical and simply bore too much extraneous ideological baggage for them. The anarchistic strain was admirable and functional representation was sound, but the rest was simply too much and, to be sure, far more antirational than almost any Englishman could bear. But if Syndicalism was excessive, Fabianism was too simplistic, the kind of ideology one might expect from a society led by a thoroughly pragmatic, hard-working, and unsentimental ex-bureaucrat like Sidney Webb.

Cole, despite his formal affiliations, was never really a Fabian. He held a high regard for some of the society's members and leaders. He shared many of their values and approaches, and certainly their life-styles. He, like them, strongly adhered to an anticapitalist stance. Cole was also able, later in life, to live with many of the contradictions and paradoxes of being a Socialist in a society that was capitalist, and was perhaps better able to understand how the Fabians had endured this. He was also able, however, to remain much less impressed with the Soviet Union and its accomplishments than were the Webbs. The Soviet state from its founding was, after all, a large, remote, and bureaucratic entity which was to be viewed by Cole with suspicion even before the records of purges and terror were to be writ large on the pages of history. The Webbs were quite unlike this. They were taken in completely, and their ecstatic praise of the Russian experiment rather easily got to the point where the Webbs no longer cared about the Fabian Society, the Labour party, or any of the traditional organizations and goals with which they had been associated.[25]

In 1915, Fabianism had simply appeared to be "too slow" to Cole.[26] It also failed to incorporate the aesthetic heritage and somewhat mystical elements of Guild Socialism. Penty's book had urged a return to the crafts of the Age of Guilds and to a belief that the worker should not be separated from the values and satisfactions that are a part of the life of a craftsman. The Industrial Age and its manufacturing processes did not provide these values and satisfactions. No sense of accomplishment was attainable for the industrial worker, and state ownership of industry could in no way, at least by itself, guarantee this. Penty and Cole did not believe that the circumstances and practical problems of modern industry would permit any kind of return to an age of craftsmen, but they did believe that alienation in the workplace could be attenuated and even eliminated through control by the workers. Production quotas, standards, methods, and procedures were to be set by the workers. Privilege would be swept away, and workers would share in the full fruits of their work.[27]

The National Guilds League was a contentious group of people. Debates at the national conferences were abrasive, with both Cole and Hobson, and the latter most particularly, engaged in a great many splittings of hairs.[28] Hobson himself has described these conferences by saying, "There is a tendency to go heresy hunting."[29] Unlike the Fabians, the NGL was shortlived. It had dissolved by 1923, and it never had more than six hundred adherents.[30] There are a number of reasons for the league's short life. One of the most important is the success of the revolution in Russia. Cole and Hobson, who of course had sympathy for the revolution but who also felt that the Soviet model was too centralized and inapplicable to British needs, could talk about the advantages, attributes, and nuances of a Guild Socialist model of society and of such attendant strategems as "encroaching control." But Lenin was not talking about a model of society which might come into being at some future time; he and the Bolsheviks had done it—they had replaced capitalism with a Socialist state for the first time in modern history and they stood for and represented a living model. This was compelling to Socialists of every variety. In the United States, for example, it accounts—along with the terrible repression of Socialists during and after World War I—for much of the dissolution of the Socialist party in the 1920s and for the birth and growth of the American Communist party. In Britain, the Democratic Socialists in the Guild movement, in the Labour party, and in all Socialist groupings were impressed with the Soviet accomplishments, and a significant number joined the newly founded British Communist party.

Another reason for dissolution of the NGL is found in the fate of a variety of guilds which were established, on a more or less experimental basis, to put Guild Socialist principles into practice before the advent of a Guild Socialist system. These guilds were formally attached to the NGL through a 1922 conference which established the National Guilds Council. This council therefore tied the fate of the league to the fate of the guilds. Hobson had much more to do with the organization of the guilds than did Cole, who had a curious lack of interest in them that may be charged in part to his distrust of Hobson.

The most important of the guilds was the National Building Guild, which constructed quality houses at cost, primarily for London and Manchester workers. This experiment worked well as long as credit arrangements for construction were underwritten and partially financed by the Ministry of Health. An abrupt change in policy squeezed the guilds' credit position and, after some unsuccessful shoring-up operations by Hobson, they became insolvent. There were also some Tailoring Guilds in Glasgow, Leeds, and London, some Furniture Guilds, a London Piano Workers' Guild which was highly successful for a time, and an Agricultural Guild at Welwyn Garden City. There may have been a few others, but all of the guilds disappeared and a recounting of their experiences by Cole indicates that no one seems to know what happened to the smaller guild groups.[31] The dissolution of the National Building Guild, on the other hand, was well known and it undoubtedly had a dispiriting effect upon the Guild movement.

III *The Twenties and Thirties*

Important as the Guild Socialist movement was to Cole and disappointing as its collapse must have been to him, he was never without causes in which to immerse himself, nor did he want for writing projects. The great upheaval of the 1926 General Strike found him setting up a University Stike Committee at Oxford which worked in liaison with the local trade-union movement. He reacted to the Great Strike with enthusiasm and great emotion. This is the only time in Cole's life that he wrote a musical revue all by himself, *The Striker Stricken* (music by Gilbert and Sullivan), a work that is still occasionally performed. One of its clear purposes was to satirically promote the strikers' point of view. The absence of a press during the General Strike had left reporting entirely to what was then a strongly antiunion BBC and Winston Churchill's strikebreaker-produced *Gazette*, and performances of this review were one of the few ways a second viewpoint could be presented.[32] The easy defeat of the strikers was difficult for Cole to accept, though his dispassionate account in the *History of Socialist Thought* does not betray his feelings.[33]

There may be a direct line between Cole's disappointments with the National Guilds League and the aftermath of the General Strike and his return to the Fabian Society in 1928. His great point of difference with the Fabians, their support of the Labour party, had disappeared. Labour had by this time come around to a Socialist point of view, establishing the party's attachment to nationalization that is today enshrined in Clause Four of the party's general manifesto. This is not Cole's idea of Socialism, of course, but he was at least willing at this time to work within a party that had set its goals and principles against capitalism.

There is no reason to suppose that Cole was somehow becoming more "realistic" or pragmatic in his approach to politics or to his social ideals. The Labour party had changed. The Fabians, well past their brightest days, were in need of Cole, his keen mind, and his leadership abilities. Cole was by this time a well-known and respected figure in social and political literature, in Socialist political circles, and in academic life. He had been appointed Reader in Economics and Fellow of University College, Oxford, in 1925 after his resignation as

Honorary Secretary of what now appeared to be a Communist-oriented Labour Research Department.

This appointment as Reader is remarkable in the light of Cole's academic background and his degree in "Greats." His strong and able conversance with economic theory was obviously taken into account. He also possessed and had demonstrated his strong acumen in working with economic data. The study of economics in Britain, it should also be remembered, has traditionally been more strongly associated with the study of politics than it has been in the United States and elsewhere. Cole's authorship of *The World of Labour, Self Government in Industry, Guild Socialism Restated*, and numerous tracts and articles by this time were also undoubtedly a factor in his appointment.

In the late 1920s Cole decided that future political action, in order to be worthwhile, should be carried out in the Labour party and with groups closely associated with the party. This could never be an entirely satisfactory channel for his efforts, and it is difficult to imagine Cole having the kind of enthusiasm for the Labour party which he had shown for the Guild Socialist movement. The grudging compromise necessitated by joining such a slow and uninspiring organization symbolized a lack of satisfaction and a source of tension which Cole experienced in this association. The tension in this relationship would remain with Cole for the rest of his life, for the pragmatic appearance of a few of his actions and the pragmatic sound of some of his words could tend to mislead the uninitiated and might move them to ignore the idealism which always motivated his thoughts and actions. The years 1925–1930 also saw an intensification and continuation of G. D. H. Cole's work with the Workers Educational Association and the beginning of his association, as a contributor, to the *New Statesman*, a journal which played a more important role than any other in his life. Later on he would become a member of the *New Statesman* board and one of its chief guiding stars.[34]

Cole was selected as the Labour candidate for King's Norton, a Birmingham constituency, in 1930, but he resigned in 1931. This was because of health; 1931 was the year in which he found out that he had a serious form of diabetes and he was then "changed from a normal person who was not very robust to a man who was never for long out of doctors' hands."[35] This was not only a serious blow to Cole in terms of hampering his intellectual pursuits of writing and lecturing; it was also a great misfortune to the aesthetic Cole, to that true disciple of William Morris who was enthralled by the beauty of life as seen on walks through the Cotswold Hills or favorite places like Mid-Wales or Buckler's Hard in Hampshire. Sometimes he charted a course and carried an ordinance map, but often as not, he just started out with no plan at all:

. . .there is one kind of jaunt I do like—seeing England, or for that matter Scotland or Wales, or anywhere else that I can feel to be a part of my own country. "Foreign parts" are all very well for a change. But for steady pleasure give me a bit of England I haven't yet seen, and find unspoilt, or at any rate interesting. . . . The best way of seeing England is on your two feet, with a knapsack, and an entire uncertainty about where you are going or where you will spend the night.[36]

The difficulties Cole faced with his health problems made the 1930s a troubled time for him, and the politics of the 1930s were also depressing. The effects of the Great Depression, the rise of Fascism on the Continent, and the shattering of the Labour party in the wake of MacDonald's turncoat performance of establishing a National Government were all causes of a great melancholia on the Left in Britain.

Cole's work continued; in fact a retrospective look at his output shows that he worked just as hard, or perhaps harder, in periods of ill health than he did when he felt better, despite the great extra effort which was involved. As might be expected in such a great period of unrest and turmoil as the 1930s, he turned his hand to a considerable number of speculative articles on the economy, on foreign policy, and on the seemingly insuperable task of rebuilding the Socialist cause in Britain. These articles, as well as some of his books of this period, were of uneven quality when Cole's standards are considered, but of good quality when compared to any general standard. He wrote *The Intelligent Man's Guide Through World Chaos* in 1932, *The Intelligent Man's Review of Europe Today* with Margaret Cole in 1933, and *A Guide to Modern Politics*, also coauthored by his wife, in 1934, and these and similar works of this period performed an essential service of gathering facts and statistics and of explaining the background and social forces which accounted for the Depression and for the rise of Fascism.

Quite naturally, Cole was mistaken in some of his speculations, but his mistakes, considering the cataclysmic events that were taking place, were of an amazingly minor character.[37] He certainly recognized by this time the Stalinist terror in the Soviet Union and the importance of the secret police in that society.[38] He also recognized the significance of Keynesian economics at a very early date, though he of course preferred Socialist economics. He not only opposed the absurdity of the MacDonald government's policies in moving to cut wages and social welfare programs, but he pointed out how Keynes had actually scored a *coup* on everyone in the economic field—capitalists and Socialists alike—with his successful application of the principles of deficit spending and economic pump-priming. This was a significant admission for any Socialist to make at this time, but it is a clear representation of the nondogmatic character of Cole.[39] What was particularly painful for Cole in this period, though it hardly shows up in his dispassionate analyses, is the perversion of Guide Socialist and Syndicalist principles by Italy's Fascist government. The corporate state system, which recognized, in a *pro forma* way, the principle of functional representation but which perverted it by placing all authority in the hands of a strong and centralized dictatorship, was regarded by him as an insult to some honorable traditions and principles.[40] This is also the period in which Cole wrote the first edition of his book on Marx, an effort marked by dedicated scholarship which, flawed as it is on some points, has enjoyed a considerable success.[41]

Cole was very interested during the 1930s in maintaining and perhaps enlarging his position as a spokesman of the Left with an impressive following of students and activists. The Cole Group of his Oxford years of the 1920s was now branching out, with many of the individuals in the original group, such as Hugh Gaitskell, becoming important in their own right. Gaitskell would eventually become Leader of the Labour party in Parliament and Leader of the Opposition. In keeping with this personal aim, but also for altruistic reasons, Cole organized the SSIP—the Society for Socialist Inquiry and Propaganda—in the early 1930s, but this organization had a life of only two years. It was succeeded by the Socialist League, a group which fought within the Labour party against a policy of British rearmament. This point of view, placed against the backdrop of European history of this period, was obviously a mistake, but it emanated from mistrust of the Tories, a belief that their government should not be extensively armed after the repressive experiences of the General Strike and of the governments of the 1930s, and from the pacifist and antiwar traditions which have always been strong in the Labour party.[42]

Far more important than either of these organizations was the New Fabian Research Bureau, which Cole helped to organize in 1931. The NFRB, which was not joined to the Fabian Society until 1939, bore the broad stamp of the Cole Group and of the SSIP in its membership, officers, and publications. Forty-two publications, many of them written by Cole, were produced by the NFRB from the time of its founding until its amalgamation with the society; these works were in the Fabian tradition of solid research with a relatively small amount of polemics. The NFRB in fact virtually took over the task of tract publication for the society, which was *in extremis* during most of the decade. Particular attention was paid, in the tracts and in the quarterly published by NFRB, to the development of Socialism in other societies, with special emphasis upon the Swedish and Soviet models. Delegations of Fabians and NFRB people visited the two countries during this period, and Cole was able to visit Sweden and meet government officials there.[43]

Cole continued to gain strong and respectful recognition as a political figure during the 1930s. He increasingly authored the Labour party's publications, including *A Plan for Democratic Britain*, a 1939 book which must be looked upon as a part of the blueprint for British society which was later enacted by the postwar Labour government. His political presence can also be demonstrated by the bogeyman image painted of him by Tory and National candidates and by the Tory press during this period. On some occasions these sources quoted Cole in such a way that it could only be said that they were making up things out of whole cloth. He was falsely charged, for example, two days before a national election, with plans to nationalize the building societies and to thereby confiscate the savings of the poor.[44]

IV   *World War II and Postwar Years*

The years of World War II were difficult in Britain, with bombings and scarcity imposed upon everyone, and they were especially difficult for Cole. Sleeplessness caused by the noise and bombing during the raids combined with his already poor

health to cause his doctors to sentence him to Oxford for the
duration of the war.[45] At Nuffield College, which had been newly
established by Lord Nuffield (William Morris), the car manufac-
turer,[46] Cole undertook one of the most extensive research tasks
of his life—the Nuffield Reconstruction Survey. The aim of the
survey was to develop materials on the British society and
economy which could be employed in setting up postwar
planning, and to present a list of achievable social and economic
goals. Cole's philosophy would undoubtedly guide the progress,
as well as the proposals, of the survey, aided and buttressed by
the work of his research assistants, and Cole's essential belief
about the postwar period was that capitalism, in the form it had
been known both before and during the war, would be vastly
reformed or might even disappear altogether. This idea was
anathema to Lord Nuffield, and though there is some difficulty in
tracing all the facts of this controversy over the survey,
university officials noted Nuffield's "concern" at the way the
survey was going. It was also apparent that certain government
departments looked upon social reconstruction research as their
own domain, and it is suspected that this view was also conveyed
to the university. Facing this kind of pressure and well aware of
its impropriety in terms of academic freedom, Cole felt that he
had no choice but to resign from the project in 1944.[47] It is
interesting that despite this unfortunate experience, Cole later
agreed to sell his papers to Nuffield College, where the Cole
Collection is still to be found today, and also subsequently
accepted a Nuffield College appointment. All of this proved to
be very good for the College, which has achieved considerable
prestige as a center for social studies despite its relatively recent
founding date (1937) and the fact that it is easily the newest of
the Oxford colleges. The College has Cole to thank for much of
this.

Cole's return to London in 1944 was ill-timed. A bomb
severely damaged his home there, and the damage to the
structure, which allowed dampness to pervade it, had direct
effects upon his already bad health. The severe postwar power
shortages also contributed to his discomfort and to a further
deterioration of his health. He nonetheless remained active,
publishing *The Intelligent Man's Guide to the Postwar World, A
Century of Cooperation*, and some important histories of the
Labour party and of the British working class. He took an even

greater hand in the *New Statesman,* and he was appointed to still another fellowship and teaching position at Oxford in 1945, this time designated as Chichele Professor of Social and Political Theory and, later, as a Fellow of Nuffield College. Again this required separation from his wife on certain days of the week, an arrangement they had known during the war when he was at Nuffield and she was working on a number of projects, some of which were connected with her position as Honorary Secretary of the Fabian Society. Cole also served the society as its President in 1952, after having been Chairman from 1939-1946 and from 1948-1950.[48]

The relationship of Cole and the Labour party in the postwar period was, as always, ambivalent. It was satisfying to see Labour win the government in 1945. Cole himself was Labour candidate for one of the two Oxford University seats in Parliament, a kind of representation that was soon to be abolished by the Labour government.[49] The great social welfare measures in areas such as housing and perhaps more particularly in the National Health Scheme were given support by Cole, and he also supported such "big state" measures as steel and coal nationalization.[50] The accomplishments of six years of Labour government were recognized as no mean feat by Cole, and a huge percentage of the Labour representation in Parliament was in fact made up of his friends from the Fabian Society.[51] There were problems in this relationship all the same. Cole can only be said to have played a peripheral role in the development of Labour government policy, and most of his influence would have to be considered indirect through sources such as Fabian publications, Labour publications, his books, and the *New Statesman.*

The worst Labour policies, from Cole's point of view, were in foreign policy. He believed that the Labour government too often accepted the Cold War outlook of the United States. He was well aware of the difficulties of dealing with Josef Stalin and the Soviet Union, but it was also not in Britain's interest, he believed, to be aiding in those foreign-policy developments and stances which were intensifying East-West divisions.[52] This viewpoint was quite unpopular in many quarters of British public opinion at the time, including the Labour party and the majority of its adherents, but some of the newer histories of East-West relations during the postwar period belatedly tend to bear out Cole's point of view.[53]

Nor were such policies good Socialism. Cole had been, at one time or another, on both sides of the issue of permitting Communists to be active in the Labour party, but he was always single-minded about the question of Socialist-Communist cooperation. He of course opposed the centralization, bureaucracy and police–state aspects of the Soviet system, but he also was aware of a number of points of convergence between Democratic Socialism and Communism. He listed four common grounds of belief:

(1) "Essential instruments of production (must) be collectively owned and used for service of the whole of society and its people and for furthering the common interests of all the peoples of the world." All Socialists and Communists are against capitalism, the exploitation of world resources for private profit.

(2) Both share an interest in establishing the welfare state, i.e., an income floor under wages, social security, health standards, and living conditions.

(3) They also share a common belief that no one sound in mind and body has any good claim to live on the product of another's labor without contributing a fair share of his own; accordingly, unearned income of this type should be swept away, and

(4) "The main responsibility of building a new society and abolishing class distinctions rests upon the working class."[54]

These common grounds demonstrate a great deal about Cole's thinking on Socialist-Communist relations, and they help to explain many of his attitudes toward Labour's Cold War foreign policy. When the Tories came to power in 1951, he excoriated them for supporting the Americans in the Korean War. He believed that the two Koreas were artificial entities brought into being by the Cold War machinations of the two Great Powers, and the Chinese had every reason for intervening after it appeared that Truman and MacArthur were going to send troops into Manchuria. He was severely criticized for these unpopular views, but he could hardly be considered pro-Communist; he even hinted broadly that the United States and Britain should intervene on Tito's behalf if the USSR attacked Yugoslavia![55]

The 1950s, the last decade of Cole's life, were to a great extent taken up with the writing of the five-volume *History of Socialist Thought*, his most impressive work. His failing health in these years imposed severe constraints on all of his efforts. He continued lecturing at Oxford and played an important role in the continuing development of the *New Statesman*. He made his only trip to the United States as a visiting professor at Roosevelt University, Chicago, in the spring of 1958, and he also delivered some lectures in Canada and in New York. He died in London on the morning of January 14, 1959.

V   *Values and Life-Style*

The strength of his commitment and dedication to Socialism and to the variety of allied causes with which he was associated are not doubted by any of his contemporaries, though Cole's concern for the poor, for the trade unions, and for the disadvantaged cannot be traced to his origins or life style. Cole lived a life of comfort except in the years of World War II, when his health suffered because of some deprivations which can be traced to the emergencies of that period. His commitment originated in the depths of his aesthetic and intellectual experience; and of these two, the latter must be considered the stronger, though he considered them equally important. Cole said, for example, that as much as he loved the English countryside, he was willing to see it spoiled if this was necessary for the construction of decent homes for the poor and the working class.[56]

The Coles had three children, Anne, Humphrey, and Jane, and though their lives were busy and often perplexing because of various circumstances, they appear to have been basically happy.[57] The marriage of Douglas and Margaret established an intellectual partnership which was every bit as productive and impressive as that of Sidney and Beatrice Webb. Some would say it was more so, because it was a partnership which produced far more originality in political and social thought. Their life of research, reading, writing, and lecturing probably sounds more idyllic than it actually was, but there were surely great rewards in it. They found many of their joint enterprises pleasurable, and the joint authorship of their many detective thrillers was a source of light entertainment to them. Cole also expressed an interest in doing a large anthology of English poetry, and he initiated this project with his wife several times, but it never came to completion.[58]

The Coles were also ardent book collectors, and although Cole

did not read many novels, he enjoyed going over his favorites
again and again:

There are shelves and shelves of Anthony Trollope; and then shelves
and shelves of Captain Marryat, Wilkie Collins, Charles Reade, Mrs.
Gaskell and so on, even down to Charlotte Younge. . . . Henry James
still survives in full force, and of course Hardy, Meredith and
Stevenson. Gissing is there too, but most of Maurice Hewlett got
weeded out. . . . Among living writers there are mountains of Wells
and Belloc and Chesterton and of course Shaw. But not very much of
the younger generation. There are usually a lot of detective stories, but
they come and go except for a few standard authors, such as Austin
Freeman and Conan Doyle. I am afraid I just don't like modern novels,
apart from a few exceptions—which is at any rate one mercy, for
anything that saves space can be regarded as a blessing.
    . . .I have specially cherished collections—William Cobbett, Daniel
Defoe, Robert Owen, Jeremy Bentham, Jean-Jacques Rousseau,
William Morris, Walt Whitman and Thomas Love Peacock. I almost
added Karl Marx, but it is more appropriate to wear him near the brain
than the heart.[59]

Cole's love of detective stories led him to write that he strongly
opposed the classification by newspapers of fiction into two
headings—novels and detective stories. This presumes, said
Cole, that the latter cannot also be a good novel and it assumes
that all stories dealing with crime are of a single type. He
regarded Wilkie Collins's *Moonstone* as ideal detective writing;
and although he never specifically says so, there is evidence that
he thought of *Murder at the Munition Works* as the best of the
thirty-odd detective stories he coauthored with his wife.[60]
    Cole's greatest collection task, however, was in the area of
working–class and radical history. His vast amount of pamphlets,
books, clippings, newspapers, and other memorabilia contained a
great deal of fugitive material, and this is perhaps the most
worthwhile characteristic of the Cole Collection now located at
the Nuffield College Library. Cole took great delight in building
this collection, and said that his

greatest pleasure in life is lighting on something that fills a gap in my
collection in some dusty old bookshop full of rubbish; buying out of
catalogues is much less fun than getting the dust of a really dirty old
bookshop up your nose.[61]

Cole, as already noted, was a sometimes irrational anti-American who had some very close American friends.[62] His anti-Americanism was not unnatural since it was directed at the world citadel of capitalism and because a number of issues—the terms of the American loan is a prominent example—involved what he considered the greed and venality of U.S. political and industrial leaders. This does not mean that he did not respect and even like some American political innovations and institutions. He was congratulatory when he praised the CIO, the strident collection of American industrial unions, as being "to the left" of the British Trades Union Congress,[63] and his histories of labor and the working classes show considerable sympathy for various American movements.

Part of his anti-Americanism can be explained by referring to his strong antitechnology and antibigness biases. The tenure of Cole's lifetime saw the establishment of the United States as the examplar of the technological society, with its (to Cole) undesirable attendants of alienation of the worker from craftsmanship and from the workplace itself, the invention and construction of sophisticated weaponry, and tall buildings, for which he had a peculiar dislike.[64] This attitude toward America may also have some roots in Cole's Little Englander outlook, a viewpoint he carried through most of his life.

Cole occasionally permitted personal friendships to be a factor in his political outlook, and his preference for Hugh Gaitskell over Aneurin Bevan as Labour party leader is an interesting case in point. Bevan seems to be just the type of Labour leader and fighter Cole traditionally admired in the Workers Educational Association and in the Independent Labour party—a working-class trade unionist who, by sheer self-will, had become a scholarly, highly respected, and always principled leftist and Marxist leader. There is little question that he was one of the greatest leaders the Labour party had ever had, and the esteem and even adoration he enjoyed may only be paralleled by Keir Hardie.[65] But Cole and Bevan "just didn't click," [66] and Gaitskell had been Cole's student for whom he had always had great affection.[67] Cole therefore preferred and supported Gaitskell, who was the prime attacker of the party's commitment to Socialism, who stood on the other side of the unilateral disarmament issue, and who served as chief Labour apologist for NATO. On these, and on other issues as well, he stood poles apart

from Cole, although Cole was willing to tell him on one occasion
that he and, for that matter, the Labour party, had become
reactionary.[68]
Even more surprising than his preference for Gaitskell over
Bevan, when looked at within the context of his rather
anarchistic philosophy, is Cole's receptive attitude on the subject
of government service. He was a candidate for Parliament on two
occasions, once in the early 1930s and again in 1948. He would
have liked to serve the Labour government elected in 1945 if he
had been asked; he was not. His health was without doubt a
factor in this, but not entirely. He also had been a very
temporary civil servant at an early point in his career, and the
Nuffield Reconstruction Survey was quasi-governmental in
nature. His outlook and temperament have nevertheless led
Dame Margaret Cole and others to doubt that he would have
stayed long in political or governmental offices of any kind.[69]
There are a few, but only a few, sides to Cole's outlook and
personality which appear to be enigmatic. One example which
stands out is a long paean of praise for the life-style and ways of
the Tory aristocracy which Cole recited while on a long walk
with Hugh Gaitskell, but this is merely of passing interest and
could be explained by some mood which had overtaken him on
that particular day.[70] A rather famous little poem about him says
that he was a "puzzle," "a Bolshevik soul in a Fabian muzzle."[71]
Though more amusing and quaint than accurate, the verse
highlights the tension that Cole must have felt all through his
life, a quandary caused by the classical dilemma of idealism and
pragmatism. He did well most of the time in resolving this
dilemma, for there are very few who would say that he was not
effective in nearly all of his endeavors and there are fewer still
who believe that he did not stay by his principles.[72]

CHAPTER 3

Cole's Thought

THE distinct contribution of G. D. H. Cole's literary accomplishments and social thought must be largely ascribed to his Guild Socialism. The originality and prescience of *Self-Government in Industry, Guild Socialism Restated,* and other works directly related to Guild Socialist theory are of signal eminence, but this outlook also affected the host of writings he turned out long after the demise of the National Guilds League, and his insistence upon guild principles was evident throughout his life, whether he was writing about Labour government policies, international questions, trade unions, local government, or political theory.

The prescience is verified by the fact that the world is still grappling with the issues Cole set out and sought solutions for— the questions of technology's place in society, of bigness and remoteness of institutions, of distribution of wealth, and of production of wealth—and by the keen interest that has developed in applying the same, or very similar, policies, programs, and remedies that he advocated. The originality is clearly evident in Cole's Guild Socialism.

I *Characteristics and Roots of Guild Socialism*

What is a Guild Socialist? The full answer to this requires some attention to the background of influences upon Cole, the preeminent Guild Socialist, and upon such men as S. G. Hobson, A. J. Penty, and A. R. Orage; but in brief, a Guild Socialist is one who ascribes to the organization of society along the following lines:

Guild Organization. Each member of an occupational group, whether it be machinists, office clerks, or shop workers, is organized into a democratically run workplace organization, which is to be called a guild. Each guild is given authority over all matters relating to production and the goods or services in the domain of the workplace. Since direct decision-making by individuals is placed at a high premium and since coercion of any kind is considered abominable by Cole and Guild Socialist theorists, a maximization of democracy is to be established at the workplace. The only occupational "group" which has no place in the system is the capitalist class, which will be abolished. Maximizing democracy also means that in large factories or in other producing establishments workplace organizations, or guilds, will be set up on a departmental or subdepartmental basis.

Government. The central government under Guild Socialism is expected to have very restricted powers, limited to matters such as foreign policy, defense, and justice. It would be federal in organization, highly decentralized, and limited in any control it may have over the smaller and more localized units. The major representative body would be composed of representatives of the guilds, the producers in the economy, and of the consuming public, with each possessing half of the total representation. No representation is to be based upon mere numbers of people; Cole felt that this is one of the most meaningless features of Parliament. Representation, under Guild Socialism, is therefore based upon functions performed by individuals in society and not necessarily upon the size of groups with which they are associated.

The Achievement of Guild Socialism. Unlike Marxists or Syndicalists, Cole and the other Guild Socialist theorists did not believe in a violent revolution as the vehicle of achievement of power. They believed in a system of "encroaching control," in which the capitalist management—who, at the time these theories were set down, were one and the same much more than they are today—would, in bits and pieces, give up all of its authority over production, hiring and firing, the setting of standards, and all other phases of management of the firm. Since this often appeared impossible to achieve, especially to Cole, he believed that it may be necessary for the state to assume control of a firm or of an entire industry prior to its transformation to a system of workers' control.[1] This possibility is rather strange for Cole to set forth, since he worried so much about state control of institutions of any kind and since this was always a major point of contention between Cole and more orthodox Socialists.

These are the bare bones of Guild Socialism as advocated by Cole.[2] Many other features of such a system, such as the prohibition against any individual's living off the earnings of another by putting such wealth to one's own use, abolition of the wage system (to be replaced with something called "maintenance," but Cole is not sure or explicit on this point), a prohibition against excessive wealth, and an emphasis upon consumers' cooperatives and consumers' protection, are also important, but they appear, for the most part, to logically follow the conditions set out for the organization of the society, of government, of the economy, and of industry. The abhorrence of large institutions and even more of the great powers they inevitably develop is also manifested in the emphasis upon decentralized power and upon democracy at the workplace. Less obvious, perhaps, is the attitude of Cole and the Guild Socialists toward technology, mass production, and machine-oriented innovations.

Looking at this problem of technology and its effects from a point of view considered at a later time in the twentieth century, it can be said that many of the major concerns of social observers and social critics are taken up with this question. And this question, the technology question, is often thought to be broader in scope and deeper in its effects than the questions of Socialism and inequality, though it is surely linked with those questions. It accounts, for example, for New Left movements surpassing the older Leftist movements in importance during the 1960s.

Cole's concerns with the question of technology run strongly parallel to similar concerns voiced by the New Left movements, though he made his known several decades earlier, at a time when the benefits of technology were not subjected to the scrutiny typical in present-day Western society. H. G. Wells sang its praises as a part of the liberation and salvation of humankind, and political and social writings, economic analyses, popular culture, and even popular music were wedded to the idea of progress through technology. The disadvantages of technology were viewed differently as well. It was known at the time of Cole's youth that environmental damage was wrought by industry and by mechanized transport, and this accounts for the passage of laws which the environmental cause has been able to use today. This was not, however, the major source of concern, which was the dehumanization experienced by workers in carrying out mass production processes. This emphasis of social change advocates has never really abated in the entire experience of industrial societies, and recent endeavors in writing, research, and political organization are evidence of a renewed effort in the 1960s and 1970s.[3]

The modern production techniques introduced by the Industrial Revolution caused a basic alienation between worker and work. It may have been more efficient, as with Adam Smith's famous example, for one worker to specialize in production of one part of a pin while another specialized in some other part. It may also have led to a lower price for pins. But it also set the worker farther away from the finished product—more precisely, from the fruits of work—and from a sense of accomplishment, a sense of identification with work and with oneself, a sense of worthwhileness and adequacy, and a sense of craftsmanship.

These were, to Cole's mind, the most important characteristics of the dehumanization wrought by industrialism, but there was another set of factors almost as important: those related to the surroundings in which workers were subjected to such processes. Cole wrote:

There is a tract (written by William Morris)—*A Factory as it Might Be*—in which he contrasts the sordid character and surroundings of the typical factory of his own day with his vision of a factory well laid out in beautiful surroundings and not crowded into a narrow city space—a factory in which work could be carried on under healthy and pleasant conditions and the workers employed in it could live in pleasant dwellings in close touch with unspoilt country. Since he wrote a good many factories have been built, if not according to his prescriptions, at any rate in such ways as greatly to diminish both the sordidness of the working conditions and the squalor of the housing provided for their workers. But too many of the older sort remain. . . .[4]

The environment and conditions of the workplace are therefore important considerations to Cole, and it is certain that the aims of his Guild Socialist outlook are as directed to these concerns as they are to more mundane matters such as money or wage rates. (The wage system, in fact, was considered an important lever of oppression against the working class.)[5] The atmosphere of the workplace is a question of worker dignity and it is not an issue which lends itself, in Cole's view, to compromise. This question remains important today in Britain and other industrial countries; in the early months of 1974, for example, a miners' strike, which was rooted in questions of the atmosphere of the workplace, caused a major emergency and the downfall of a Tory government. The question of the workplace environment also remains paramount in most American labor unions as well as British unions.[6]

Cole of course never had the direct experience of being subject to a bad work environment, and this could be considered a handicap for one so immersed in studies and concerns of the working class. But Cole was with the working class, not of it, and his approach to such issues may therefore have less of a "common sense" base than that of working-class leaders such as Keir Hardie, Ernest Bevin, Aneurin Bevan, or others who came out of the shops, the pits, and the trade unions. Many observers may not consider this important, but the study of working-class needs and interests is one of the few areas in which direct and personalized experience yields useful general insights and perspectives.[7] This is doubly significant in the case of the Guild Socialist movement, for it did not fall victim to any snobbish or self-centered elite leadership at any point; it learned a great deal from its working-class members and leaders and from their experiences, which taught them to reject capitalism and any and all of its promises.[8]

Cole was able to make up for a lack of any direct experience with his strong sense of vision, and this is also a necessary ingredient for any Socialist movement. Utopian frameworks must be sketched out in the works or at least in the minds of Socialist advocates in order to know what directions and incremental gains to work toward; this was one of the great miseries of the New Left movement of the 1960s, for almost everyone involved in it knew what they were against while seldom knowing what they were *for*.

Cole was always well aware of what he was for, although his explicit ideas, plans, and manifestoes display, at one time or another, a variance with general Guild Socialist principles on a few points or nuances. In the main, however, it can be said that he was generally influenced by these Guild Socialist principles, traditions, and methods:

Intellectual leadership. The National Guilds League was strongly influenced by Fabian methods and tactics. The League, after all, had many ex-Fabians like Cole in it. This meant an attachment to fact-gathering and research, to the giving of lectures, and to publication of tracts and other propaganda.

Encroaching control. Believing that the General Strike idea and the idea of the "myth" and its creation by the workers were impractical encumbrances of Syndicalism, the guild movement adopted the idea of "encroaching control." Thoroughly imprac-tical and unworkable as well as holding a special place as the Achilles' heel of guild argument and outlook, this idea is posited as a belief that the employer class will voluntarily agree to a piecemeal alienation of its authority and that, over a period of time, this class will bargain itself out of existence. The Guild Socialists can probably be accused, with some justification, of thus dropping one piece of ideological excess and replacing it with another.

Pluralism. Not to be confused with the "pluralism" or "polyarchy" which are sometimes used as descriptive terms for the American political process, the term in this case applies to a belief that the plurality of groups in a society, whether they are manual workers, domestic workers, or professionals, must and should be represented in the decision-making bodies which are established by society and that this representation rests upon function or, in other words, upon the councils elected at the workplace.[9] Consumers as well as producers are to receive representation, though their voice will be heard at the level of government through representative institutions. Pluralism, then, is an ideal which recognizes that each of the diverse interests which characterize any society must have a voice in democratic decision-making. In Cole's Guild scheme, the guilds, which are the workplace and shop organizations which establish democ-racy in the workplace community, are to be coequal with the state.

Primary importance of production. Despite the provision for representation of consumers and all other interests (save, of course, capitalists, owners, or managers) in the Guild Socialist society, the primary emphasis rests upon the producers' com-munity, which achieves its political and economic expression through the guilds. This was not particularly in Cole's design, but his theoretical work nonetheless yields this effect.

Cooperative movement and medievalism. Guild Socialism weds two important intellectual and social currents of the nineteenth century—producers' cooperatives and the medievalist movement. The latter, which has been humorously treated in the Gilbert and Sullivan operetta *Patience,* was an antitechnology and indeed antiscience revolt fostered by men such as John Ruskin, who emphasized the glories of craftsmanship and workmanship and who abhored mass production techniques. William Morris, the greatest of all intellectual and aesthetic inspirations to Cole, was a disciple of Ruskin. The reformism and idealism of the cooperative communities such as the Owenites of Lanarkshire match those of the medievalists, and this tradition has also been carried on through much of the history of cooperatives in Britain, a history which Cole knew well and wrote about. The Owenites believed in the replacement of capitalism with a utopian society in which producers' cooperatives would be the dominant social and economic organizations; moreover, they practiced what they preached, setting up a Grand National Guild of Builders, which was very much like the Building Guilds established by the Guild Socialists in the 1920s. These two important traditions of medievalism and the cooperative spirit find their way into Cole's writings at many points and in many books, but they are also shown in his choices of Robert Owen and William Morris as subjects of two of his works.

Pre-Marxian utopian Socialism. The influences of the medievalists and of the cooperatives are both characterized by strands of Socialism of a utopian and pre-Marxian brand. A Socialism which tends to look more at the ideals of the society which is sought and which is to be created, rather than a Socialism which emphasizes and rests upon class distinctions or upon a doctrine of historical inevitability, is the goal and emphasis of Cole's writings and of the traditions which were most important to them. This is also a Socialism that took root in the minds of people and philosophers many centuries before the rise of the Industrial Revolution. It probably goes back as far as Augustine.

Anti-Parliament attitude. This utopian outlook, because it tends to deemphasize questions of political strategy and tactics, also tends to look upon politics as a somewhat tawdry business. It is believed by some observers that this accounts for the anti–Parliament attitude of the Guild Socialists—this is certainly a strong theme in Cole's work—but Parliament also had little place in a scheme in which authority would be decentralized and would devolve upon small units such as workshop organizations. This opposition to Parliament did not, however, stop Cole from seeking election to it nor did it deter him from admitting the need for some kind of national representative body even under the Guild Socialist scheme. This opposition to Parliament primarily consisted of objections to its overpowering supremacy in British government rather than in terms of objection to *any* representative scheme. Cole realized that Britain was large enough to require an indirect representative body of government.

The values and methods implied in these criteria and traditions—intellectual leadership, encroaching control, pluralism, the primacy of production, the cooperative spirit, medievalism, utopianism, and an anti-Parliament attitude—succinctly set out most of the influences that were important to the development of Guild Socialism as advocated by Cole. There are nuances, differences associated with personalities, and other factors which require exploration, but these are certainly the most important criteria and traditions which affected Cole and the National Guilds League.[10]

The league never could list quite the cast of luminaries of the caliber of the leading Fabians. S. G. Hobson did some distinguished work for the league and has left a significant monument of himself in the form of the houses built by the Building Guilds, but he was hardly considered to be in any intellectual category similar to that of the leading Fabians or to that of Cole. Cole was the guild movement's chief thinker, theoretician, prophet, and definer of guild principles, goals, strategy, tactics, and purpose. Some famous names—Bertrand Russell, Ivor Brown, R. Page Arnot, Will Dyson the cartoonist, George Lansbury, and R. H. Tawney, for example—were associated with the guild movement and may have been members of the National Guilds League, but their membership and support was, for the most part, nominal.[11] It should not be concluded from this, however, that the impact of the guild movement was small or insignificant. The movement held a considerable attraction for Christian Socialists, for some ex-Fabians, and for Communists until the latter formed their own party. The leaders of the guilds movement were strategically placed in a number of influential roles and positions:

This earnest, tiny group (a few hundred in all the Kingdom) appear in various service uniforms and play many parts. As university graduates, they are at the heart of the University Socialist Federation. As Christians they are Church Socialists, sapping the Established Church. As Guildsmen, they conduct a league, honeycombing the unions. As investigators, they are the Labour Research Department, affiliated to important members of the trade union movement. As Fabians, they buffet Sidney Webb. As journalists, they have entry to powerful newspapers and weeklies.

As writers, their books—*Self Government in Industry* and *The Payment of Wages*—are . . . irreplaceable because of the careful collection of facts and the understanding of currents of tendency. But their great service has been that of agitators with a smashing generalisation.[12]

Cole contributed mightily to Guild Socialism and to British Socialist traditions generally through his iconoclastic approach to political and social questions. It is not easy to tie Cole to the major currents of British political thought in the way, for example, that the Webbs can be shown to be creatures of Benthamite tradition and of the great English liberal tradition. Cole was neither a traditionalist, at least in that sense, nor a liberal, and he was not one to reconcile himself to these general currents. He was able to reconcile the important and sometimes competing currents which underlay Guild Socialism, but some of these currents—Syndicalism being the prominent example—are not British in any specific sense. He was willing to accept those strands of political thought and points of view which could make Socialism a greater force in Britain, but he was neither able nor willing to compromise with what he found to be the prevalent currents of the British outlook which persisted through most of his lifetime, for he was too utopian for that, antirational to some degree and rather romantic, even though he was also a thinker who employed the Hegelian dialectic and a nearly omnicompetent intellectual who chose to dabble in whatever happened to interest him at the moment.

The individual is an obvious reference point of Cole's political beliefs and ideals, but his interest and concern for the individual tend to be understated. He probably would not understand, for example, John Stuart Mill's categories of self-regarding and other-regarding actions and the distinctions between them, and he was wholly out of sorts with Adam Smith's belief in a highly individual entrepreneur. Cole's concern for the individual is manifested in antipathy toward big government and big corporate enterprises or, for that matter, any instrument (including, on occasion, trade unions) designed or used for oppressive purposes. The individual's role, when assessed by Cole in terms vis-à-vis institutions, is defined in terms of the individual's interest. It has occasionally been alleged, because of this, that Cole's reference point was the group and not the individual. But everyone in modern societies has some kind of interest, whether as a producer, craftsman, tradesman, consumer, or whatever, and this interest can generally be viewed in collective, rather than individual, terms for purposes of setting social policy.

This is Cole's pluralism, a plurality of interests of varied sorts, all acting as useful producers in the community. This pluralism has less application on the consumers' side than on the producers' side, since it appears to be assumed that consumers' interests will not vary considerably and since it is further assumed that all producers are carrying out their work for the benefit of the whole community. This latter point is a significant departure from Syndicalism, one of the important sources of Guild Socialism, which assumed that the work of the community was carried out only for the benefit of the working class.[13]

Cole's pluralism must also be distinguished from the pluralism set out by sociologists and political scientists as a description of modern Western societies, especially the United States and Britain.[14] This outlook is only vaguely, if at all, cited as an ideal and this is totally unlike Cole, whose pluralism served as one of the building blocks of an ideal society. Descriptive pluralists such as Robert A. Dahl, Nelson W. Polsby, or Seymour M. Lipset attempt to set out a model which tells how society works.[15] Competing interests set out their views in this model and, most importantly, their demands on governmental systems. The competition of demands and viewpoints leads to a process in which compromise is achieved by "grinding down" the various demands to a point of decision. The simplest example might be a labor demand for a minimum wage of three dollars, a business demand that it remain at two dollars, and a decision in which the minimum wage is set at two dollars and a half. Less simplistic examples are more generally used, however: a deferred demand is made stronger two years later simply because it has been deferred, one interest has more economic and/or political potency than another, or a compelling moral argument figures in the equation. In any event, compromise is achieved, the system proceeds along more smoothly as a result, a kind of approximate or appropriate justice is brought about through this process, and every interest recognizes that it has a greater stake in the system itself than in their particularistic demands. The system is, of course, a capitalist system in the form now prevalent in Britain, the United States, and other Western societies.

The pluralism of Cole and the Guild Socialists is similar to this model in that the interests of each group are given a hearing, that they make demands which may compete (although it is assumed that this is less likely to occur in a Socialist society), and that each group has a greater interest in the functioning of society than it has in the insistence upon meeting its particular demands. The differences in these two pluralisms, however, are greater than their similarities. In the first place, Cole and the Guild Socialists would not call the Dahl-Polsby-Lipset model "pluralism." Pluralism has only existed in Western societies as an ideal, and it does not describe any capitalist society. It may have limited application to phenomena such as Owen's experiments or other communal societies, but even these were subject to a framework of capitalism since they had no real sovereignty of their own. A capitalist economic system, furthermore, does not establish a system of equal competing interests. Pluralists such as Dahl readily admit this, but they are all the same committed to the idea of access; that is, they believe that almost every group or interest at some point has access to the vital decision-making processes of a political system. Socialists almost never accept this, and Cole and the Guild Socialists certainly did not. Capitalist systems, said Cole, are dominated by an acquisitive spirit which is inimical to any process of economic or social justice. The system of rough justice which the descriptive pluralists claim is a natural result of the interaction of competing demands is, Cole would say, rough indeed.[16]

Socialism became a part of Cole's creed almost as soon as he heard of its existence, and the uniqueness of his Guild Socialist outlook did not imply sectarianism or compartmentalization.[17] Cole has written extensively of, and implied even more extensively, the need for unity of Socialist movements of various kinds. This is shown in his support for the principle of Socialist-

Communist cooperation, believing that the differences of these two great tendencies are less important than the principles they hold in common. This is further shown in the feeling he had that he and his Guild Socialist associates and his Fabian and Labour party associates were the heirs of a long tradition. This tradition included the Chartists, the Owenites, most certainly the Marxists, and movements as far back as the Levellers and the Diggers.[18]

The Chartists are singled out in a number of the works of Cole because, however unwisely they may have been led at times, they were a signal movement for reform with their demands for suffrage, the secret ballot, and the facilitation of the election of the poor to Parliament. They were also interesting to him because they contained within their movement a number of tendencies and sources of disunity, including the agrarian-based, anti-industrial followers of William Cobbett.[19] This is quite in character for Cole, for the Anti-Corn Law movement, which can be set out as distinct from the overall reformist thrust of the Chartists, contained within it the kind of antitechnological and even antiscience bias which is found in his Guild Socialism.[20]

The Owenites were not much different in this respect, for Owen became convinced very early in the nineteenth century that the entire basis of the industrial system was wrong and that competition in profit-making necessarily involved misery for the mass of the people.[21] Cooperative societies and a general cooperative system were considered to be the substitutes necessary to deal with the excesses of capitalism, and Owen was one of the early developers of a critique of capitalist theories of value and in this sense was a forerunner of Marx.[22] The period around 1830, just a few years before the first great electoral reform, was one in which the terms "Owenite" and "Socialist" were virtually synonymous, and experiments such as the Owenites carried out at Rochdale were guided by a belief that a cooperative structure of the economy would supplant capitalism.[23] The Owenites, like the Guild Socialists ninety years later, were visionaries and were skeptical of industrial and technological innovation, especially if such innovation meant—as it had in the cotton industry—the elimination of any interesting or creative tasks for workers as well as reduction of their wages and worsening of their working conditions. The Owenites also believed that they had found responsible and workable answers to capitalism; in their own lifetimes, they had seen the dissolution of the Luddite movement, which had declared all-out warfare against machinery and technological innovation. Cole and the Guild Socialists demonstrated a parallel responsibility in recognizing the impossibility of a return to a pre-mass-production age, despite their intense aesthetic attachment to the ideas of craftsmanship; this difficulty, they realized, would have to be met by changing the structure of the political and economic systems as well as of the industrial system, by humanizing the workplace, and by finding and affirming the workers' sense of accomplishment and, through this, the workers' sense of identity in mass society.

Cole and the Guild Socialists also owed a large debt to Marxism. Cole has been described as a Marxist, but all Marxists stand for their own unique brand or blend of Marxism.[24] If Cole was a Marxist—a question open to considerable doubt—he certainly served as proof of this, for his Socialism was indeed unique. But Cole did not consider himself a Marxist. He employed dialectical thinking processes, he believed in the working class and in its ability and perhaps even its destiny to rise to a tremendously improved position through an alteration of political, economic, and social structures, but he also believed that the great significance of Marx lay in his unique ability to stress (and, as far as Cole was concerned, to prove) two points: the fact of the exploitation of the working class under capitalism, and the eventual (though not necessarily inevitable) victory of the working class that should and could be attained over capitalism. [25] Cole defended Marx against Orthodox economists, and he believed that nineteenth- and twentieth-century Britain was not the kind of atmosphere in which Marx could or would receive the credit due him. Brought up on Oxford "Greats" including Hegel and Kant, he had learned to strongly dislike deductive philosophy, but he was not concerned with stressing the many points upon which he disagreed with Marx. He was more interested in defending Marx and in crediting him with his great contributions to social thought. He disliked any fraudulent attempts to rewrite history, and he therefore opposed the Stalinist version of Marx's historical role as well as this version's interpretations of Marx.[26] Marx fought oppression, and would cringe at its use in his name. Like Marx, Cole insisted that the victory of the working class over capitalism must be total. The results of this victory, according to both Cole and Marx, must be revolutionary, and must therefore involve the supplanting of the capitalist ownership class with a system of social control. The method of reaching this victory, however, was different with Cole. He set up "encroaching control" in which the capitalist would, through a series of stages, negotiate himself out of business. Marx was willing, though he advocated a variety of methods in his lifetime and was never a dogmatist, to remove the ownership class through a violent revolution.

II Cole's Approaches to Politics and Society

It is obvious, however, that Cole's theoretical work and praxis diverged. Cole lived and worked within the framework of British society and government, and these institutions were the most stable in Europe if not in the world. Nearly all of the Continent had been rocked by revolutionary forces in the nineteenth century, especially in the convulsive year 1848; France had its Revolution in 1789; but Britain had developed a tremendous stability since the time of its much earlier, preindustrial revolution in the Cromwellian era. British society, moreover, held values and traditions which were inimical, indeed fatal, to the idea of revolution, and Britain, however horrendous some of the conditions of the working class might be, was a country which instituted reforms, believed in social progress, and was able, in the nineteenth and early twentieth centuries, to be optimistic about the future. Cole knew that he was more dissatisfied about social conditions in Britain than most people were, or more importantly, than most articulate people were; therefore it was not possible for him to be a full-fledged Syndicalist or Marxist. Perhaps the closest that Britain has come to a revolution in this century was at the time of the General Strike of 1926, but this was a long way from it and, as Cole has pointed out, the results and aftermath of this event were reactionary.[27] Therefore, Cole was forced to embrace a gradualist approach to social change, especially after the General Strike, and was required—as much as he thoroughly detested doing so—to endorse Fabianism on tactical grounds.

The major reason for this gradualist approach is that, as much as he had reservations about such organizations as the Fabian Society and the Labour party, Cole thoroughly detested capitalism, and it was better to be rid of it through a gradualist process than never at all. This would require, of course, a policy for dealing with an economy in which Socialist and capitalist enterprises exist side by side, and Cole did set out the frameworks for just such a policy.[28]

Coming around to such an outlook was a long and tortuous path. Cole tacitly admitted the continued existence of capitalist enterprises in his Guild Socialist theory, for the idea of "encroaching control" was based upon this, at least until such time as all capitalist institutions could be swept away; but this tacit admission was not the same as going to lengths to see that capitalist enterprises made sufficient profits so that unemployment would be no problem, a concern which was set out by Cole in 1957.[29]

What is capitalism? More precisely, what is capitalism in terms of Cole's understanding of it? It is a system of private ownership which

assumes the general right of a man to do what he pleases with "his own," to use his capital, however acquired, whether by luck, enterprise or sharp practice, in employing other men, who are without capital (proletarians), and to pocket a part of the proceeds of their labour. Such employment of one man by another, whereby the capitalist owns the product of the worker's labour, is called "exploitation." It diverts the value created by one man to the use of another, merely because the one has capital and the other not.

This is wrong and unjust, not because every man has a right to what he produces (which is the crudest individualism), but because no man has a right to any property unless his right is consistent with the well-being of the whole community. Capitalism is, in short, the charter of the licensed profiteer.[30]

Abhorrent as the system was to Cole, he had no desire to put capitalists to death or, for that matter, to put them out of business except upon the rather gentlemanly "encroaching control" basis.

Cole and the Guild Socialists were not primarily concerned with the capitalist, however; they were concerned with the working class, though they perceived it in non-Marxian terms. It was this concern and this movement—Guild Socialism—which account for most of Cole's original contributions to thought on political and social change through gradualism. It was Cole who gave this movement its central direction, its most sophisticated theory, its social blueprints, and its leadership. Cole was not only the leading intellectual light of Guild Socialism, but was also the major leader of its "center tendency," the largest group in the Guild Socialist movement and the group which most strongly resisted other tendencies in the National Guilds League. These other tendencies were Communism on the Left and Douglas Credit on the Right. Since these two tendencies contain elements which are antithetical to guild ideals and were therefore threats to the movement, it can also be said that Cole and his supporters, who represented a majority of guild followers, were also the most loyal to the general guidelines of Guild philosophy.

The Douglas Credit group deserves very little attention. The number of its adherents was quite small, although A. R. Orage of the *New Age,* one of the founders of the guild movement, came round to it.[31] The scheme, originating with one Major C. H. Douglas, was based upon a credit system which would increase the buying power of everyone without essentially transforming the society or dealing with such questions as ownership and distribution of capital. It was the forerunner of "funny money" counterpart movements in Western Canada and in New Zealand, and it figures in the founding philosophy of the Social Credit party, which ruled both Alberta and British Columbia for several decades. This party was soon transformed into a populist version of Toryism, paradoxical as such a description may seem, for it favored and promoted reactionary economic policies while ignoring its founding traditions. Leaders of this party today look embarrassed and proceed to change the subject whenever any "funny money" questions are asked of them.

The Communists were another matter. There was nothing approaching a majority position for them within the National Guilds League, but they were a minority of significant size. They left the guilds movement altogether upon the founding of the British Communist party and they had a profound impact upon the dissolution of the guilds movement. They also placed immense difficulties in the path of G. D. H. Cole:

I found myself in a difficult position in the post-war years, for I was a left-wing Socialist who was never at all tempted—as many of my friends were—to go over to Communism, because I entirely disagreed with its fundamental approach—as I did indeed with the Labour

Party's. For the basis of my Socialism was a deep belief in the value and free will of the individual, and I heartily disliked any mass movement that seemed to me to underrate or deny its importance. I was against centralism whether it manifested itself in the dictatorship of a class—or of a party supposed to represent a class—or in an overweening advocacy of the claims of the State as representing the whole body of citizens. I believed that democracy had to be small, or broken up into small groups, in order to be real, and that it had to be functional for this to be possible—that is, related to a definite and particular activity and not to an indiscriminate medley of purposes combined in a single body deemed to be superior to and different in its motives from all others. To this conception of democracy I have adhered all my life. . . .[32]

This is a good and succinct statement of why G. D. H. Cole could never be a Communist, but it also pinpoints those concerns which led him to be a Guild Socialist: the belief in small government and the belief in functional representation.

The belief in small government, which is antithetical to Communism and especially to the Soviet model, was a persistent theme in Cole's writings, statements, manifestoes, and principles. "Nowhere," the Utopia designed by William Morris, has no set number of citizens, but Cole strongly inferred that it was a small society blessed with very small government.[33] The correlation of bigness and coercion runs through Cole's thought and work with such persistence and strength that it tends to surprise those who associate Socialist writers and theorists with a belief in big government.

Cole went to great lengths to distinguish Guild Socialism from Communism. The circumstances wrought by Stalinism eventually made such a task even less difficult, but he nevertheless felt compelled in the early 1920s to set out these distinctions: (1) "encroaching control" rather than violent revolution;[34] (2) Guild Socialiam is an ideal because it looks toward a new society while Communism is not an ideal, but only a method, since it sets out the means for achieving power "without defining the nature of the society to which it looks forward;[35]" (3) the obvious difference of limited government as advocated by the guild movement, versus centralized control; (4) the differences in terminology used by the two movements. Cole, like the Communists, believed in working for and supporting the demands of the working class, but he believed that the term "working class," as well as terms such as "soviet," or "workers' republic," did not really mean very much other than a repetition of the Communists' major proposition that all power must be in the hands of this class and that little else matters; in other words, these terms were only incidental to Communist method and did not define the society they sought; (5) tactics and approaches to immediate needs; the Communists, for example, told the workers and other followers that unemployment would always exist until capitalism was abolished while Cole and his adherents urged action to combat unemployment even if this should have no connection with the establishment of a society along Guild Socialist lines, and—just as importantly—Cole always favored the establishment of welfare state measures on health, pensions, and unemployment benefits even though he recognized that this might make capitalism more tolerable;[36] and (6) lastly, Cole believed that revolution was not acceptable to the vast majority of the British people, who were steeped in institutions and political processes which held stability in high esteem. This is not the only consideration in this objection, however, for Cole tended to take a dim view of apocalyptic change. He admonished Socialists to be constructive and to be able to build new institutions as old ones are scrapped.[37]

This last point also demonstrates a number of reasons why Cole was eventually willing to work through the Fabian Society, the Labour party, and other reformists, rather than revolutionary groups. Immediate relief of the workers and the poor through the ameliorating effects of welfare-state measures was a good and reasonable goal of political action in Cole's eyes. A better today rather than a better tomorrow was considered a politically sound approach. Once again the question of pragmatism is raised, but this is pragmatism only in the sense of achieving more or less immediate benefits for the poor and oppressed; this, too, is Cole's idealism, as well as his humaneness, on view, but it yielded him only a measure of satisfaction. This approach also blends well with some of the reformist impulses of his Guild Socialist movement, which always demanded the elimination of unemployment and want along with its recurrent demands for self-fulfillment in the workplace.

III   *Criticisms of Cole's Guild Socialism*

Cole and the Guild Socialist movement—they at times appeared to be one entity—were seemingly always embroiled in political disputes with other groups on their Left and on their Right. The fractional disagreements with the Communists and the Douglas Credit advocates have been alluded to, but Guild Socialist theory as enunciated by Cole has also been subjected to criticism from other Socialist and non-Socialist sources. Some of the criticisms can easily be dismissed, such as some of the nasty but insubstantial swipes taken at Cole by various writers and intellectuals. Harold Laski and Max Beloff are two who fit this category.[38] There are also some general denunciations of Socialism which, for purposes of this study, are not very important. The Conservative party in Britain, for example, has generally maintained that it is self-contradictory to establish an "authoritarian" economy without the use of force. Either one must renounce Socialism and return to "freedom," the Tories have said, or there must simply be the employment of more and more force, and the tendency for Socialists is to do the latter.[39] This criticism, as one might guess, is more directed at the orthodox and Big State Socialists with whom Cole had little sympathy in any event, although it must be added that Cole would explain that there is a basic fallacy in this argument because of its equation of freedom and capitalism. To Cole, freedom was only possible in a Socialist society, and the idea that political freedom had any meaning in the absence of economic freedom was callous and unworkable.[40]

A rather similar but perhaps more substantial criticism is directed specifically at Guild Socialism by the right-wing economist Ludwig Von Mises. After pointing out that "Guild Socialism represents the one contribution to modern Socialist plans made by the Anglo-Saxons,"[41] he asserts that Guild Socialism fails—just as all other forms of Socialism do—to transcend the problem of state control. By setting off the guilds, which control industry, against a consumer-controlled government which regulates wage and price policy through the taxing system against industry, Cole has hoped to avoid the difficulties and evils of centralization. This is not the case, according to Von Mises, because control of production still belongs to the state through its economic power. The fact that state control is indirect does not alter this. The guilds, he prophesies, would be relegated to the position of merely executing the will of the government. Guild Socialism asserts a federal economic system and this is made with some reference to a federal political system, but organization of production is quite a different matter. Cooperation of local officials is important in administration, but society cannot leave it to workers to control production. The state will therefore closely regulate production, and even though the directors and foremen of such industry are chosen by the workers, they would still have to assert the same zeal as those not so chosen or production will decline. Therefore, according to Von Mises, Guild Socialism does not surmount the difficulty of establishing a Socialist order of society. It merely disposes of the distasteful term "nationalization."[42]

The difficulty with this criticism appears to originate in Von Mises's general preoccupation of criticizing orthodox Socialists. He set out a wholly new format when he stated that society will not leave it to the workers to control production and that the state will therefore regulate production. This is not Guild Socialism, and the Von Mises criticism from this point on is directed at something other than what Cole had in mind. There is also a technical point which should be raised here: Von Mises, who apparently did not understand Guild Socialist theory well, discussed the application of wage rates even though Cole and the Guild Socialists strongly advocated the abolition of the wage system. Cole was never quite sure about what kind of system would replace wages, but he was certain that "wage slavery" had to be abolished.[43] The major criticism set out by Von Mises, directed at producer–consumer conflict and the intervention of the state, was answered by Cole when he stressed the necessity of dealing with this problem:

Though there is no likelihood of antagonism, there is likelihood of misunderstanding; and the best remedy for this is that producers and consumers should be able to meet and discuss their respective standpoints and wishes.[44]

This is, after all, perceived as a Socialist society, which means that exploitation of one person by another will have been abolished and in which good will can therefore be assumed. Cole and the Guild Socialists were more concerned, however, with criticisms from other Socialists, not only because they tended to respect such opinions a great deal more, but also because these were voiced at the time when the movement was making a substantial impact upon the political and economic life of Britain. Communists were among the principal critics, but criticisms from the Left generally followed these lines:

Guild Socialism is a fraud on the workers because it promises to eliminate the capitalist while it retains capitalism. It patches up the wages system with maintenance, instead of showing that wages, or the price of labour power, must always be but a mere fraction of the wealth produced by the workers.

Guild Socialism promises betterment for the workers here and now, and an easy transition from Capitalism to Socialism. Already their chief concern is for the financial success of their business contracts [Guild loans] and not at all for education of the workers in Socialism, without which there can be no transition, easy or otherwise.[45]

This criticism is thrust upon that ever-weak aspect of Cole's scheme, "encroaching control," as well as upon the Guild Socialists' always queasy establishment of a substitute for the wage system. This is not a criticism Cole could easily answer, since Guild Socialism of course eschewed revolution and since the answers on replacement of the wage system were different at different times. The criticism is well placed, settling on the vulnerable chinks in the guild armor and especially upon the naiveté and impracticalities of "encroaching control." In a certain sense this argument also demonstrates the effectiveness of some of the Communist arguments which, played against the background of a new and living experiment in Russia, ultimately helped to lead to dissolution of Cole's Guild movement.

Some of the more important criticisms of Guild Socialist theory and of Cole's interpretation of it are made by Cole himself. He stated, many years after the movement's demise, that he had held too many illusions about the transformation of the trade union movement into a mechanism which would be more amenable to Guild organization.[46] He further came to recognize in later years the impossibility, given the times and circumstances, of obtaining Guild Socialist goals; but this, it should be remembered, is only an admission of some tactical errors. There is no evidence that Cole ever had regrets about setting out Guild Socialist theory and devoting himself to its cause.

IV   Cole's Commitment and Definitions

A distinction must be made between Cole's commitment to Guild Socialism and his commitment to general principles of Socialism. The latter appear to be more evident in his writings dating from about 1930 onwards, for he had a tendency after this period to drop off the "Guild" adjective and referred to himself merely as a "Socialist" much more often, and—perhaps owing to his reaffiliation with the Fabians—he occasionally referred to himself as a "gradualist."[47] Cole took the time, on several occasions, to testify to his continued fidelity to Guild Socialism. On many more occasions, however, he attempted to define, as well as advocate, Socialist principles in general terms. The influence of William Morris is still very much in evidence in these definitions, but Cole makes it obvious that he is not attempting to be sectarian and that he is seeking to broaden the appeal of Socialism.

An understanding of Cole necessitates a fathoming of his answer to the question, what is Socialism? His definition includes a consideration of the elements of Socialism, which include democracy, both political and economic, cooperation, the control of private business, public ownership of industry and services, security from want, an internationalist point of view (developed from the late thirties onward), anti-imperialism and anti-racism, and social planning.[48] Socialism is a cause for the working class, but it does not exclusively belong to it. Cole believed that it crossed class lines and that ultimately it must be considered good for all groups in a society.[49] The traditional elements of his outlook are also contained in this definition, for it included the requisite of no alienating elements between workers and their work. Socialist society should attain, and is capable of attaining, this attitude towards the workplace because all work is to have meaning and is to be organized in such a way that workers receive the full fruits of their labor as well as satisfaction in carrying it out. There is no Benthamite "greatest happiness of the greatest number" in this formulation of Socialism, as was the case with Fabianism and the Webbs. The happiness and well-being of all is sought.

This happiness and well-being depend upon the relationships which people develop, one with another. Fellowship, according to Cole, is the first principle of Socialism, and this principle requires that human beings treat each other as ends in themselves and not as means. This fellowship is therefore tied to political, economic, and social justice. The difficulty, he stated, is that social habit works against this, and social habit is rooted in differences of wealth as well as national, racial and other differences. Capitalism therefore has a self-perpetuating mechanism working for it. The dominance of a "spirit of grab" provides some individuals with a rationalization as well as with a self-protective instinct which thrusts them into these self-perpetuating mechanisms of the system. These problems and differences can be overcome, but the fact that they can be overcome makes them no less an obstacle. Fellowship is not an altruistic sentiment, for if it is merely this, it can already be said to exist. It is rather the transcendance of the barrier of the divisions of society into classes and races and the substitution of the rule of consent—in all aspects of society, including the political and economic—for the rule of coercion. In one sense, all Socialists regard Anarchism as the ideal, for coercion is an evil.[50] The pursuit of fellowship and the absence of coercion in society are, however, only some of the ingredients of human happiness, and so the principles of Cole's Socialism are

. . .not a complete way of living. I distrust the man for whom the Socialist ideal, or any other ideal, looms so large as to cover the whole of life. For that, I think, is a sign of inhumanity; and Socialism is above all a creed for ordinary men. Love of humanity does not submerge other loves—of wife, or children, or friends; indeed, these other loves are fires to keep it warm. Socialism is for me, I think, the most important single thing that exists. But I am not sure even of that. And I am quite sure that it is not the only thing that matters.[51]

The nondogmatic view of Socialism which characterized the stance of Cole rings crystal clear in this passage. What his Socialism was about and indeed what Cole was about is well illuminated by it and provides a fine-edged insight into his thought.

Some of the more general elements of Cole's attitude toward Socialism are also shown in the writings he undertook for the Labour party in the 1930s and 1940s. Cole never failed to look for common ground with other Socialists, and he was at least slightly impressed by the fact that, in addition to state ownership, Labour sought other forms of industrial and services control through cooperatives and through municipal ownership.[52] Cole also stressed, in a book which he wrote for the Labour party, that economic changes, particularly in the structures of dominant firms in the economy, had set up a different kind of choice both for himself, with his Guild Socialist qualifiers, and for the general public. The choice for Britain, said Cole, was not between Socialism and competitive capitalism. That form of capitalism was no longer important. Instead, the choice was between Socialism and monopoly capitalism.[53]

Important segments of industry were nationalized and British welfare state services were established by the Labour government of 1945-1951, and though Cole supported Labour at this time, he also saw some of his fears about orthodox Socialism come true. In some industries, nationalization did not achieve all that had been anticipated. The coal industry, for example, was in bad shape at the time it was taken over, and the government could not provide it with necessary technological improvements or even with adequate safety standards. Cole's articles reflected deep concern over this and similar shortcomings of Labour policy, and he and other observers stated that the miners believed their new employer was as bad as their old ones had been; moreover, the history of the industry in the past three decades has been an unhappy one. Dockers and railway workers have had similar problems and discontents, and like the miners, they have experienced great dissatisfaction, to say nothing of the complete lack of any type of industrial self-government envisioned by Cole. Despite the problems with specific industries and services, however, the general planning for industry and for services that was carried out by Labour was often quite successful; interestingly, this portion of the Labour program had been advocated by Cole.[52]

Less than euphoric about some of the experiences and problems faced by Socialists with a Labour government, Cole appeared to despair of the party altogether after its successive defeats of 1951 and 1955. He had always been scornful of some of its organizational features such as the Annual Conference, where a few trade-union leaders cast a majority of the votes and there appears to be no cognate relationship with democratic theory or practice.[55] But he was now looking well beyond such considerations and taking a broader and indeed worldwide point of view. It would no longer do to be a Little Englander, to simply concentrate upon the achievement of Socialism in Britain while ignoring the plight of others in the world. What is more, such a policy would, according to Cole, be an exercise in futility. The Labour party was not leading Socialists to anything but more of the same game of Parliamentary politics. He occasionally identified with the left-wing branch of the party, its extra-Parliamentary associations such as the Campaign for Nuclear Disarmament, and its advocacy of unilateral nuclear disarmament and of continued fidelity to Socialism,[56] but this appeared to provide only a meager satisfaction.

Cole considered the dilemma of the Labour party. It lost ground in the 1955 elections. The outlook for Socialism, as well as a policy of advocating it, appeared to be losing ground, but support of welfare-state measures and their extension, which he viewed as the other alternative, would also be ineffective because the Tories could do the same and could—who knows?—perhaps administer such welfare programs as well or better than Labour could. Socialist parties in other countries, particularly in Western nations, were confronted with the same dilemma and were also, generally speaking, out of power. One fact remains, said Cole. Socialism was "still a good cause with a good case,"[57] and it was still a cause with wide appeal. Capitalism, on the other hand, was inimical to worldwide cooperation and therefore unable to make the best use of world resources, and capitalism should also be considered immoral since its basis could be described as one of encouragement and strengthening of greed and acquisitiveness.[58]

Cole therefore proposed what he called a World Socialist Crusade, based on dedication to a worldwide cause rather than to national political parties, though he still considered these important. He simply felt that political parties could not lead in this. They could only follow through once the groundwork was laid by a great ethical movement. He knew that in this proposal he was inviting the label "utopian," but he felt it was even more utopian to expect people to vote for a Socialism they did not want and which political leaders of the Left knew they did not want and therefore did not expect to be able to produce.[59] This proposal led to Cole's formation and leadership of the International Society for Socialist Studies in 1956, although he could not give this organization his full-fledged support and attention because of the severity of his health problems. This dimension of Cole's thought is particularly important, since it is a near-abandonment of the Labour party as a vehicle for social and political change and, most importantly, for Socialism. His support for Labour from this point on must be considered rather limited since he felt that no national political parties could play a leading role in the development of Socialist theory or of Socialist societies.

Subsequent events have borne out a number of Cole's analyses. In the case of the Labour party, it is safe to say that he would not have been happy with it when it finally returned to power in the period 1964–1970. No international crusade for Socialism developed quite in the way envisioned by Cole, but a revival of the Left was felt around the world in the 1960s, and this revival and its effects consumed great attention in Britain, Western Europe, North America, the developing areas, and even in the Soviet Union and Eastern Europe, notably Czechoslovakia, where the equation of Socialist economics with democratic political systems was, for a time, strongly set out. In no case did this Left revival come about through the efforts of, or associations with, the traditional political parties of the countries concerned. In Britain, West Germany, the United States, Canada, Italy, Spain, Australia, or wherever else the revival took place, it took a nonparty, extraparliamentary, extragovernmental form and it transcended national boundaries, all just as Cole had felt and had said it would.

Cole also clearly foresaw the need for the development of new approaches to the world and its problems through the updating and elaboration of Socialist principles. He pointed out, for example, that a great deal of the balance of power in the world would shift to those countries which control the production of raw materials and commodities such as oil, copper, various other minerals, and food.[60] The fact that the world and the developed nations are now faced with this set of circumstances but at the same time lack any smooth mechanisms for adjustment to it is a testament to Cole's well-placed concern for a worldwide ethical movement to which such mechanisms and adjustments could have been related. Resolution of conflicts now developing over resources may take military forms instead, a thought that Cole, a strong advocate of peace and of unilateral nuclear disarmament, would have found abhorrent. Britain, and much of the rest of the world, can therefore still benefit from Cole's insight, and could— even at this late date—enshrine his wisdom in public policies.

CHAPTER 4

The Major Works of Cole

I T is difficult to select a mere handful of books from the 150 or more which G. D. H. Cole wrote and to set them out as his major works. This is nonetheless attempted in the belief that an examination of five of his major works in some depth will yield a better understanding of Cole as a writer. Since no two persons are likely to agree on what constitutes his major works, a bibliography is also being provided, and a brief listing of signal efforts and an indication of their impact and usefulness can be found at the end of this chapter. Two of his most original major works are *Self-Government in Industry,* in which Cole first set out the principles and some details of Guild Socialist theory, and *Guild Socialism Restated,* written three years later, which updates, amplifies and only slightly revises his views. The importance of these two books is self-evident since they deal with the most original and unique aspects of Cole's thought. It is also necessary, if one is to really understand Cole, to review one of the many books he devoted to the broader topic of Socialism, because it is this subject which inevitably leads to the basic moral and philosophical positions of Cole. *The Simple Case for Socialism* has been chosen for this purpose, because its essential clarity and forthrightness have made it a strong and exceptionally worthwhile declaration of Cole's political faith. In large measure this is due to its stated methods and purpose: to justify Socialism from a moral and philosophical point of view. *The Meaning of Marxism* has also been selected for analysis, though with some misgivings. The development and logic of this rather slim volume fail at a number of points and allow an uninitiated reader to perceive Marx and Marxism in rather strange ways. Part of the problem is that Cole criticizes Marx on logical, empirical, and scientific grounds. This is all very well to a point, for Cole used empirical methods in carrying out a good portion of his research and writing, but it also leads to difficulties because Cole is basically a romantic, indeed spiritual, Socialist at heart and cannot fairly ascribe irrationality or "pseudo-science" to Marx and his followers by calling Marxism a collection of flat assertions. *The Meaning of Marxism* is nonetheless a unique study of a topic which is important to Socialists and non-Socialists alike, and it is particularly useful in analyzing Cole's thought since it tells a discerning reader as much about Cole as it does about Marx. It therefore provides helpful insights in reading and analyzing other works of Cole. In addition, it has been acclaimed for provoking thought on Marxism from a Western and libertarian point of view which recognizes the humanistic side of Marx. The fifth and final major work selected for analysis is the five-volume *History of Socialist Thought,* a monumental contribution which is likely to be on anyone's list of Cole's major achievements.[1]

I Self-Government in Industry

Cole's second book, *Self-Government in Industry,* is the first that he wrote after becoming a fully committed Guild Socialist. Written in 1917, it was preceded by *The World of Labour* in 1913, in which Cole set out a more general Socialist outlook and called for the establishment of a cooperative commonwealth; he was obviously moving in the direction of Guild Socialism in *The World of Labour,* but his viewpoint was not as well refined as in his second book, nor does the first book contain the richness of insight, straightforwardness of purpose, and lucidity of the second.[2] *Self-Government in Industry* is the first book to put Cole into touch with the working class, for it was written against a background of industrial strife in the period which began during World War I and which led to the great confrontation in 1926, the General Strike. Hard and severe questioning of the nature of the trade-union movement, its structure, and its direction were ongoing concerns at this time. Cole took part in the discussions and debates on this issue, one that is at the center of the interests and concerns of the British working class to this day, and the thoughts and views he developed are set out in this "bible" of Guild Socialism. It reached a remarkably wide working-class audience.[3] Its publication, combined with his

leadership role in the National Guilds League, account for his
initial entry into nationwide fame as well as the beginning of a
long tradition of Cole as bogeyman to reactionary political
interests and the Tory press. What was important for Cole,
however, was that *Self-Government in Industry* firmly established him as a friend of the working class and as an innovative
mind dedicated to social change. The blueprint for British
society which emerged from it has strong traces of Owenite and
William Morris influence, but it is primarily stamped with the
mark of the young, idealistic, and creative Cole, who takes on
and demolishes with relish the suppositions, prejudices, and
myths which surrounded British politics, economics, and industrial life at that time and offers an alternative system. Most of the
insights on, and criticisms of, the organization of society supplied
by Cole in this volume have application beyond his time and
remain—save for some isolated experimentation in Britain,
Yugoslavia, and Sweden and in a small part of the plywood
industry in the United States— untried and untested.

A new edition, edited by John Corina and containing his
instructive introduction and notes, was published in 1972, and
Corina states that the reason for the new edition is Guild
Socialism's "relevance for today."[4] Corina regards *Self-Government in Industry* as a profound statement of human rights in
industrial society, as important for its age as Tom Paine's
manifesto of human rights was for his; but in the American and
Russian revolutions which Paine's and Cole's work preceded,
society went on to build decision-making structures which
ignored the profound prescriptions of these writers.[5]

Using the engineering industry—the British equivalent of the
U.S. machine, machine-tools, and metals industries—as an
example, Cole sets out, in considerable detail, how a Guild
Socialist system of workers' control could be organized.[6] This is
perhaps the least interesting part of the book; far more
important are the facts, schemes, opinions, and details which
Cole describes as they pertain to the state, the relationship of the
guilds to the state, the question of representation, the roles of
consumers and producers, the future of trade-union organization
and industrial relations, and the changing attitudes of society.
Cole also grapples with the sticky Guild Socialist problem of
what is going to replace the wage system.

This work is, perhaps most of all, a telling critique of what

Cole calls "collectivism"—the orthodox Socialist movement, represented most of all by the Webbs, which advocates state control of industry and services. He often refers to this mainstream Fabian viewpoint as one of "national management" or "nationalization," which he distinguishes from "socialization" of industry, the term which he feels is reflective of Guild Socialist goals and purposes. *Self-Government in Industry* is also a petulant and irreverent piece of work, mirroring not only the stridency of its young author, but also showing his willingness to take nasty but humorous swipes at various antiguild persons and groups. The Fabians, of course, are not spared; he makes the term "Fabian" synonymous with "damned." Trade-union bureaucrats are described as "Glendoveers" as Cole alludes to the verse: "I am a blessed Glendoveer/'Tis mine to speak, and yours to hear." A nasty jab is also taken at the *New Statesman*, which he regarded as a voice of collectivism, and Sidney and Beatrice Webb are dubbed "Sir and Lady Oracle."[7]

The guild theory of the state is not set out in complex detail, but the "partnership" of the guilds and the state is demonstrated through a balancing of the powers of Parliament by a National Guilds Congress. It is a system in which democratic decision-making intrudes at every point—national, regional, local, works (factory), department, and workplace.[8] Democracy is of course regarded by Cole as economic as much as it is political, and, to this extent, British democracy is considered incomplete:

Political Democracy is accepted because it has so largely failed: it is the very fact that it has not made effective the will of the individual citizen that has caused the opposition to it to die down. The fear of many of those who oppose industrial democracy is that it would be effective, that the individual would at last come to his own, and that, in learning to control his own industry, he would learn also to control the political machine. The day on which he learnt that would certainly be a black day for the bureaucratic jugglers in human lives whom we call statesmen—or sometimes New Statesmen.[9]

Cole was historically accurate. In 1867, a Tory Prime Minister, Benjamin Disraeli, had broadened the franchise in Britain, and he had done this with no fear that this extension would mean the end of control of the economy by the British elite classes. Later reforms of the election process were viewed with similar equanimity. Full democracy, therefore, is considered by Cole to be feasible only through a system of workers' control, and it cannot be achieved with private or with state control of the means of production. State ownership is in fact the last refuge for the capitalist class, since this class will be content to clip the dividend coupons provided by the state as it spends decade after decade paying for the property it has taken over once the injustices of capitalism are exposed and understood.[10]

The system of national, regional, and local guilds, coupled with Cole's insistence upon workers' control, raises the question of sovereignty of the state. But Cole will not allow himself to be drawn into the conundrums of sovereignty, not only because the complexity of its justification goes well beyond the purview of the book, but because he has no interest in establishing any such justification. Instead, he subjects the state to a demystification process, and the anarchic sweep of his prose has its effect: neither he nor his reader is left with any sense of the awe that is supposedly wrought by the subjugation of one group of human beings by another in the name of sovereign authority.[11] A state must do more than merely exist and authority must have some purpose beyond the execution of power. Additionally, Cole presumes throughout his discussion of the state that the burden of proving the need for the exercise of power rests squarely upon those who seek to justify such a need and upon those who exercise power. The corollary—that those who seek systemic social change must not be as burdened as those who support the *status quo*—also holds. The presumption must always rest with those who seek change because it is impossible to know that which has not been tried.

Cole does not subject the authority of the state to his critique in terms of class issues and dimensions in *Self-Government in Industry* as much as he relies upon attacking the basis of representation. The geographic basis of representation is alleged to be a holdover from feudal times, when there was a strong identification of an individual with a given territory.[12] This ties in closely with the outlook of the Big State Collectivists who urge and support nationalization on the basis that public ownership is in the public interest because the public is a "consumer" society. Everyone is a consumer, and therefore—the traditional Fabian and collectivist argument goes—nationalization benefits everyone. This consumer rationale is consonant with a geographic basis of representation in Parliament or in any representative body. It completely overlooks the role of producers, who cannot possibly be represented on a meaningless basis of geography or territory, but must be represented upon a functional basis. Guild Socialism, according to Cole, deals with the fallacies of both the collectivists, who emphasize the consumer side of life and activity, and the Syndicalists, who only look at the producer side when they advocate one great superunion which holds all decision-making authority.[13] Cole writes:

Guild Socialists recognise that neither the territorial nor the professional grouping is by itself enough; that certain common requirements are best fulfilled by the former and certain others by the latter; in short, that each grouping has its function and that neither is completely and universally sovereign.[14]

The powers of Parliament, which he calls the "supreme territorial association," are therefore to be set off by the powers of the National Guilds Congress, the supreme functional association, and this balance is also expected to operate at the municipal and regional level.[15]

The ownership of capital, under this arrangement, rests in the state and a transitional period of "national management," or nationalization, will be required in some industries before these can be turned over to guild organizations.[26] The major point of Cole's theory of the state, however, rests upon the recognition of the dual roles— producer and consumer—inherent in each individual, and upon the enhancement and protection of the interest of individuals as they fulfill these roles. Again the pertinence of Cole's pluralism arises, and his critique of the twin fallacies of collectivism and Syndicalism on this question addresses itself well to the needs and interests of individuals in their associative capacities.

Cole has no worries about the problem of paying off the capitalist class after it has relinquished its ownership of capital to the state. This is simply not to be done, for it would retain economic inequality, provide a burdensome debt for the state to assume, and protect unjustified earnings and privilege.[17] Cole's view, as expressed here, is much more attractive to many Socialists than it is fifteen years later when he devotes a considerable amount of thought and worry to this question and seeks a way out for the state so that it can pay the capitalists off with as little strain upon its financial position as possible.[18] The earlier view demonstrates that Cole would support some Castroite solution such as thousand-year or ten-thousand-year bonds; the later view is close to "nationalization by purchase," which he eloquently condemns in *Self-Government in Industry*.[19]

Notice is taken of the traditional opposition to Guild Socialism emanating from the trade unions and from the Labour party, and Cole's critical attitude toward these organizations and his rather low opinion of them shows through in a much more direct and unambiguous way than it does in his post-1930 writings. The Labour party, which defines the political positions of the unions to a great extent, is considered by Cole to be an ill-conceived creature of the trade unions and the Fabians. The latter can be particularly blamed for this, for they failed to enlarge Socialist theory as they perceived it to include the entitlement of the unions to control of industry; instead the unions were simply recruited to do the bidding of the Fabians in their quest for collectivism.[20] To Cole, this was a tragic lapse in reason, in logic, and in terms of tactical considerations. "The final result we know: it is a Labour Party of which Capitalism has long lost all fear."[21] The Labour party's opposition to workers, control schemes of any kind continued for fifty years until 1968, when a tepid statement of support for this principle was finally adopted.[22]

Cole's treatment of the relationship between trade unions and the Labour party reveals the complexity of analysis required for understanding this subject. This is neither new nor unique; the literature on the relationship between trade unions and Socialist parties in Europe demonstrates this well.[23] Cole makes a major mistake in his analysis of this relationship when he falls into the rather common pit of describing what the trade union movement *should be* rather than describing what it *is*. This can be expected in any blueprint which seeks to construct a new society, which *Self-Government in Industry* surely is, but it is not very helpful and is too utopian because it is easier to reform even governmental institutions than it is to reform and remake trade–union organizations. Changes and new emphases within trade–union movements must come from within, and it is nearly impossible for an "outsider," even one so distinguished as Cole, to set out any prescriptions. The best proof for this is Cole's statement, made several decades later, that he was wrong to expect the trade-union movement as constituted in 1917 to serve as the vehicle for the construction of a Guild Socialist society.[24] The collectivists, and most particularly the Webbs, are equally guilty of setting out prescriptions for the trade-union movement, however; and Cole quite willingly takes them to task for their view of unions as mere "organs of criticism" under state-ownership-of-industry systems. This view trusts the state too much and gives too little power to the unions, and Cole's misgivings were borne out by experience, decades later, when the dissatisfying and indeed melancholy state of the unions under state-run industrial systems proved his point correct.[25]

Cole's prescriptions for trade-union reform and for industrial organization, however foolhardy they may have seemed at the time and however ill-received they were by some of the unions, are vital parts of his Guild Socialist theory. He believed in industrial, rather than craft, unionism, and he supported the establishment of workshop, rather than branch, organization. His advocacy of industrial unionism sought to take nothing from the crafts or from an emphasis upon craftsmanship; it would be fair to say that the reverse—an enhancement of crafts and skills—was in fact a partial objective. Nor did Cole seek "One Big Union" as the Knights of Labor had pushed for in America. Industrial unionism was simply a tactical consideration. The trade-union movement was split into too many small units because of craft unionism. A union, or sometimes a multiplicity of unions, existed for each craft, and this meant that a typical employer was confronted with a variety of unions with which to bargain. This also meant, by and large, that there was little emphasis upon the protections and needs of unskilled workers. Even the Amalgamated Society of Engineers, one of Britain's largest unions in 1917 and a forerunner of the Amalgamated Union of Engineering Workers of today, was only an amalgam of skilled trades unions and did not seek to organize all the workers in the engineering industry. A multiplicity of small craft unions was considered unworkable by Cole in both capitalist and Guild Socialist systems.[26]

Industrial unionism also carried with it, in Cole's view, a necessity for workshop organization rather than organization of unions into branches based upon mere geographic location, and this change in trade unionism still has generally not taken place.[27]

The absence of workshop organization of unions tends to grate Cole in two ways: geographic organization and representation systems are archaic throwbacks to feudal times, and the directness, responsiveness, and representative character of organizations is compromised by their removal from the scene of immediate concern—in this case, the workshop. Unions must take the workshop level into account, for it is here—and no place else—that matters affecting industrial relations, working conditions, and the quality of the workers' environment have the most salience and take on the greatest importance. Shop stewards, who also are employees in the workshop but who take on a significant and often militant leadership role, are more in tune with workers' demands and needs than branch officials or union bureaucrats can hope for; moreover, workshop organization has much more potential from the Guild Socialist point of view than a mere reform of trade union and industrial structure. It is the first step toward the abolition of capitalism and the establishment of Guild Socialism:

> . . . we, in our day and generation, shall succeed in overthrowing industrial capitalism only if we first make it socially functionless.
>
> This means that, before capitalism can be overthrown, there must be wrested from it both its control of production and its control of exchange. This done, the abolition of its claim to rent, interest and profits will follow as a matter of course.
>
> The obvious striking point for labour today is the workshop. The assumption by the Trade Unions of workshop control would not destroy rent, interest and profits, but it would be a shrewd blow struck at the roots from which they spring. This is its fundamental import for Labour at the present time.[28]

This is the beginning of "encroaching control," in which there is a step-by-step abandonment by the ownership class of all of its control and claims. Revolutionary Socialists scoff at such an idea, and rightfully so; and Cole himself had little to say for "encroaching control" in later years even though he always preferred a heavy emphasis upon workers' control of industry and especially upon workshop organization.[29]

Another weak link in the Guild Socialist armor is the urging of abolition of the wage system, or "wagery," or "wage slavery," as they liked to call it. Their opposition to the wage system was another fundamental point of difference with collectivism, although Cole and other Guild Socialists have never made it entirely clear what they would replace it with; "maintenance," the supposed replacement, is not defined. The criticisms of the wage system listed by Cole in *Self-Government in Industry* are four in number: (1) it separates the worker apart from the work which he or she provides, "so that one can be bought and sold without the other"; (2) and as a result, wages are paid to workers only when it is profitable for the capitalist class to employ them; (3) the worker, in exchange for a wage, surrenders all control and all voice in the processes of production; and (4) the worker, in exchange for a wage, loses all claim upon the product of his or her work.[30] All of these degradations and depradations of the capitalist system must be abolished, so that workers can control the processes of production and exercise a claim upon the product of their work and, in addition, receive payment whether they are employed or unemployed, sick or healthy. The fundamental principle behind all of these requisites is recognition and reward of workers as human beings rather than as mere possessors of work power.[31] The weakness of the assertion that the wage system must be abolished and replaced by a more humane system rests rather obviously upon a lack of spelling out alternatives; the moral case is certainly strong enough.

Part of the problem lies in defining objectives, and Cole is usually clear and precise in this effort. Cole eschews the traditional idea of "efficiency" in industry or in the economy, for example. It is an idea which evokes the images of time studies, piecework, and Stakhanovism.[32] Cole redefines efficiency by saying that the "key to real efficiency is self-government; and any system that is not based upon self-government is not only servile, but also inefficient."[33] Efficiency in its traditional form also is contrary to the principles of beauty in life, including industrial life, which William Morris has so eloquently expressed. It is of the same cut of cloth as the growth syndrome which has been pervasive in Western economic, political, and social thought, both capitalist and Socialist, and which has led to human, social, and ecological disaster. The spate of "urban" and "environmental" problems which we seek to control today, and the congeries of interrelated and nearly nonsolvable dilemmas which they pose, can be found at the end of a straight line originating at the altar of mammon in the form of growth, efficiency, and technology.[34]

Efficiency and growth, as Cole and William Morris, among
many others, recognized, are at odds with the dynamic of Eros,
the latter being that part of human thought and action which
entrusts itself and its instincts to art, literature, architecture,
music, love, beauty, and the construction of societies in which
the spirit of these is dominant.[35] The growth syndrome is also a
convenient escape for those who do not wish to be confronted
with social conflict and the need for change. Growth and
efficiency are heralded as ends in themselves and, held to be
above conflicting value systems and points of view, they carry a
"spurious primacy" over the fundamental questions raised by
Guild Socialists and other social critics.[36] Addressing this central
point of Cole's stand, John Corina states that the "objections to a
present-day application of Guild *theory* have become far less
formidable than they once seemed."[37]

This leads to the major goal of Guild Socialism and of Cole as
he wrote *Self-Government in Industry,* and it is an ambitious
one: it is nothing less than to change the moral basis of society.[38]
This is a far greater task than the Fabians ever set for
themselves, and it rings with the ideals and enthusiasm of a
utopian. But is Cole really a utopian? He appears at times to be
one, but he knew very well, he said, that no Utopia is really
achievable. Some problems will always be with us—sickness,
conflict, and, in some cases, just bad luck—but Guild Socialism
seeks to do something about those problems which are capable
of solution. Cole's utopianism therefore describes the tenor and
spirit of his writing and of his philosophical approaches to his
subjects rather than his actions, his concrete proposals, or his
praxis. A heart-and-head dichotomy therefore tends to present
itself throughout *Self-Government in Industry.*

II   Guild Socialism Restated

Anyone who is familiar with Cole's basic theses concerning
Guild Socialism or anyone who has read *Self-Government in
Industry* will find *Guild Socialism Restated* to be somewhat
repetitious. The latter, published in 1920, three years after the
appearance of *Self-Government in Industry,* principally adds
nuances and emphases that did not appear in the earlier work;
and though *Guild Socialism Restated* is sometimes detailed in its
outline of a grand social design, it is altogether a succinct

statement, prosaic at times but well written and economic in style. Like all of Cole's works of advocacy—as opposed to his more objective histories and biographies—it has a conversational tone and style and is sprinkled with interjections and personal pronouns. Cole tends to avoid the imperial "we" or the impersonal "one."

An example which sets out these characteristics is found in a discussion of industries and small firms which may choose to remain independent of the National Guilds. He does not insist upon their affiliation because he believes that valuable experimentation and creativity may thereby be lost. "In insistently refusing to carry their theory to its 'logical' conclusion," writes Cole, "the Guildsmen are true to their love of freedom and varied social enterprise."[39] The emphases of decentralized decision-making and of an almost anarchic disregard of organizational thrusts for conformity extend, then, even to the guild cause and its organizations. At this point Cole continues to converse with his reader:

Moreover, I at any rate, if I can see the Guild system firmly established in the main industries, feel no anxiety that the forms of organisation which survive or are created in the rest of industry will be out of harmony with the Guild idea. Above all, I would let alone, and leave with the greatest possible freedom of development, the small independent producer or renderer of service, leaving it to the future to determine how far the services in which he is engaged are naturally led to adopt definitely Guild forms, or only to bring their organisation into harmony with essential Guild principles. An attack on the independent producer in the interests of large-scale organisation would be a fatal step for the Guild system. . . .[40]

Cole goes on to say that this anticoercive principle of nonaffiliation would apply equally to the professions, to small workshops and craftsmen, and to various trades such as agriculture and distribution. The guild spirit of craft excellence may indeed, Cole asserts, prove strongest in these areas.[41]

Clear and readable social science, though it was not as rare fifty years ago as it is now, is one of Cole's obvious accomplishments. This is probably due in part to Cole's preeminent humanism and to the touch of romanticism evident in nearly all of his writings, and these in turn are rooted in his education, his personality, and certainly in his times. Quite unlike current or "modern" social-science writing or even the writing of such contemporaries as Harold Laski, the work of Cole is always jargon-free, unpretentious, occasionally witty, and antidoctrinal. Cole therefore convinces without compulsion, explains with patience rather than stridency, and spurns dogmatism by adopting clear lines of reason. This passage, with its "live and let live" tone surfacing invariably alongside Cole's sets of principles and plans, is a rather typical example of the prose of *Guild Socialism Restated* and, for that matter, of the totality of his works of advocacy.

Guild Socialism Restated can be more properly classified as a "government" text or "political science" work to a greater degree than most of Cole's books. A few stretches of the imagination could even place it in the category of public administration or organizational behavior, since it deals with the guild scheme of government in more explicit detail than any of his treatises.

It begins with the premises of freedom and democracy as these are understood by Cole. These will be familiar at this point: the emphasis upon small decision-making units, the need for democracy to extend to economic as well as political life, the relationship of a Socialist ethic to freedom and democracy, and the need to abolish the remote and elitist traditions of capitalism, Parliament, and collectivist theory. At an early point in this discussion Cole finds, erroneously of course, that these ideas are supported by various tendencies in industrial life and strife which point to some kind of developing Guild Socialism.[42]

He also ties Guild Socialism and its need to the history of its predecessors, the medieval guilds:

The theory of State omnicompetence has grown up gradually. Locke. . . regarded the State, not as "sovereign" in the sense now attaching to the term, but as strictly limited in function and capacity. There was a time. . . in the Middle Ages, when institutions and associations all. . . exercised. . .a recognised social power and authority. During the period which followed. . . these other bodies were for the most part either swept away or reduced to impotence; but the effect of their disappearance was not. . . the assumption of their powers by the State, but the passing of the social purposes which they had regulated outside the sphere of communal regulation altogether.[43]

This in turn cleared the way for an unbridled structure of

industrial development, the results of which remain to this day: intervention by the state as a protective set of measures for the people, and this has

led to the confrontation of. . .man by a greater Leviathan, and produced a situation extremely inimical to personal liberty. . . .[44]

The implacable foe of all of this manipulation, bigness, and authoritarianism is Guild Socialism. It faces no "problem of arbitrating between divergent interests. . . . There can be no real divergence of interests. . . ."[45] The body of producers and the body of consumers are, for all practical purposes, the same people; there would therefore be no economic warfare, as in capitalism, but a reasonable democratic organization of society on a functional basis.[46] The role of producers is carried a step further than the analysis of *Self-Government in Industry:* not only do the collectivists overlook the role of producers, but they also fail to heed or demonstrate the totality of Socialist consciousness that is developed by linking producers in a complementary way to consumers. The experience of Western political systems since the 1920 publication of *Guild Socialism Restated,* as well as our increased sophistication and awareness in dealing with the phenomenon of interest groups, tend to show that Cole was wrong or too hopeful in assessing the chances for a clash of competing producer and consumer interests. Under capitalism, Socialism, or even Guild Socialism, there is no evidence that an accommodation of these interests would be either easy or automatic.

Cole moves directly into the problem of organization in Chapter 3, "A Guild in Being." Again functionalism comes to the fore, not only as an organizational format but as a unifying communal force:

I strongly suspect that the managers in. . .a Guild factory would have no cause to complain of lack of power. If they wanted authority, they would find ample scope for it; but I believe most of them would soon cease to think of their positions mainly in terms of power, and would come to think of them instead mainly in terms of function.[47]

At the very core of Cole's thought is his attitude toward humankind, as this excerpt shows, and the major formulation is that people can be trusted to turn to and use their best instincts if they are given an environment in which trust and good will are given full reign. Cole is not unrealistic or misguided on the foibles and avarice which can be found in human affairs. He even believes that human nature is probably more important than environment in determining conduct; he nonetheless believes that environment is fundamental, far-reaching, and capable of tremendous benefit for all in its effects.[48]

The basic structure of society, according to *Guild Socialism Restated*, calls for three branches of economic and social activity. The first of these are the producers' organizations— Cole also calls them "economic Guilds"—which are the best-known feature of Guild Socialist plans and which are outlined, using the engineering industry as an example, in *Self-Government in Industry*.[49] The only notable addition to this part of the framework worked out in this book is the Agricultural Guild. The second important grouping is consumers' organizations, made up of consumer cooperatives and what Cole calls "Collective Unity Councils." These two primary groups—producers and consumers—are placed on an equal footing in a national legislative body. They are supplemented by an important third grouping which would obtain less representation in the overall scheme than the other two: the civic services, which would be organized into "Civic Guilds," and the Cultural and Health Councils, which would regulate the "Civic Guilds" with a membership derived from these guilds as well as from the producer and consumer branches.[50]

All of this would fit into a highly decentralized and federal structure. Regional governments, presumably more powerful than the national government on economic matters and perhaps on all matters save national defense and foreign policy-making, would be organized along the same lines. Government is to be most effective (and therefore most important), however, at the ward (or neighborhood) level. Cole refers to ward-level government as "the Commune."[51]

"The Commune" unites the groupings at the most local level, and this requires coordinating the work of the totality of activities . . . producer, consumer, and civic . . . that are set out in the Guild scheme. The Commune's functions are to allocate resurces between each of its constituent groups (a strong tradition of pluralist ideology), provide a court of appeal for any grievances brought before the commune, determine lines of demarcation (i.e., jurisdiction) between various functional bodies, control matters concerning the commune as a whole, such as town boundaries or the construction of a town hall, and provide law enforcement.[52] All of these tasks are to be fulfilled in a spirit of Socialism and cooperation. Health and educational services, for example, are infected by greed and acquisitiveness under capitalism, but they would actually solve problems and provide good and reliable roles when they become a part of the commune and are regulated by the various civic representation bodies.

This work is the most detailed explication of Guild Socialism as an organizational model that is in existence. It is all the same compressed, according to Cole, on such important matters as the transfer of powers to the workers. His naiveté on this point is matched by his expectations for the Soviet system, since he doubts that it will remain bureaucratic. The inspiration of the revolution moves him to say that "Guild Socialists, like all true Socialists, must be internationalists."[53] This is a rather curious statement in light of the development of Cole's thought over the next two decades, though it conforms in certain respects with his post-World War II attitude.

One of the most interesting questions posed along the way is, "Who will do the dirty work under Guild Socialism?"[54] Cole points out that some Socialists have always favored a period of industrial conscription for everyone. Cole opposes this

first, and most of all, because I do not want Guild Society at any point to be based on sheer coercion, but also because I am sure that the system would operate badly and unfairly. It is, moreover, unnecessary. Let us first by the fullest application of machinery and scientific methods eliminate or reduce to the narrowest limits all forms of "dirty work" that admit of such treatment.[55]

Cole is not always antitechnological; when he sees the possibility of worker liberation in any sense, he supports innovations with tools and machinery. Secondly,

let us see what forms of "dirty work" we can do without, and make up our minds. . .that, if any form of work is not only unpleasant but degrading, we will do without it, whatever the cost. No human being ought to be either allowed or compelled to do work that degrades.[56]

Lastly, Cole would reverse the economics of any "dirty work" which remains but which must be done, "not in higher pay, but in shorter hours, holidays extending over six months in a year," so that individuals would undertake such work voluntarily.[57]

Guild Socialism Restated, despite such sentiments, is the closest Cole comes to sketching in all of the organizational requisites for a new society. For this reason it appears to be more pragmatic in its approach than *Self-Government in Industry* or *The Simple Case for Socialism,* which tend to dwell upon the human requisites. It also demonstrates, in an occasional nuance or shading, Cole's still greater disenchantment with British trade unions. Despite its importance as a landmark of Cole's thought and of Socialist thought and experience, it is more difficult to obtain than Cole's other best-known works and it deserves, like *Self-Government in Industry,* a new edition, for it is one of the best expressions of Cole's thought ever set down.

III   The Simple Case for Socialism

A Marxist or Syndicalist or perhaps any sectarian Socialist would consider *The Simple Case for Socialism* a sectarian work, and to some degree they would be right, for G. D. H. Cole is still found to be espousing Guild Socialist principles in portions of this book even though its publication date is 1935, when more than a decade had passed since the demise of the guild movement. *The Simple Case for Socialism* is nonetheless a more broadly based appeal for Socialism than Cole's early works, and its limited sectarianism is therefore of comparatively minor importance. Its major purpose is to present the Socialist case from an ethical rather than economic or political viewpoint, and, generally speaking, Cole succeeds in this quite well.

The Simple Case also contains some Cole treatises on education and culture, the state, the class system, capitalism, and the debate between Marxist Socialism and Utopian Socialism, providing some provocative insights into Cole's mind and heart. Cole uses these subjects as an effective backdrop in setting out an ethical definition of Socialism, which he believes must include an end to all class distinctions, the common ownership of the means of production, an obligation of all to serve one another to the best of their capacity in promoting a common sense of well-being, and a system "in which no one is so much richer or poorer than his neighbours as to be unable to mix with them on equal terms."[58] Britain is his obvious point of reference, but Cole places some of this work in an international perspective. He supports Socialism for every country in the world, taking exception to the Stalinist idea of "Socialism in one country," and urges that each country find its own way to Socialism, based upon the conditions and circumstances which it may confront.[59] This may appear to be a common sensical proposition today, with the varieties of Socialist experimentation now occurring in Cuba, China, Yugoslavia, Scandinavia, Tanzania, and other countries, but it was not a consensual idea within the Socialist movements of Britain and Western Europe in the 1930s and it has yet to be accepted by most sectarian Socialist groups, whether they be Marxists, Maoists, Democratic Socialists, Titoists, or whatever.

Cole insisted upon a broad measure of toleration among Socialists at all times, and *The Simple Case* is no exception. He decries heresy-hunting.[60] He instead urges enthusiasm and support for Socialism, and he insists that Socialism is very much a matter of the heart, that emotion as much as intellect is necessary for Socialist movements, and that extremists—but not gradualists—are fortunate in one respect: that they have a vision of the kind of world they wish to see created.[61] What is most important is that Socialists maintain their comradeship, recognizing their underlying unity. Cole asserts that this unity has been better achieved historically than in the case, say, of Christians.[62] This unity is required because, as he points out in a chapter entitled "Where the Shoe Pinches," the difficulties in bringing about the realization of Socialism are overwhelming. Every facet of life is suffused with capitalist morality—property ownership, church piety, obeisance to the state, artifices of class and privilege, and media control and brainwashing of the general public by the rich.[63] It is quite inconvenient even for those committed to change to break out of these conventional boundaries: the manager of the cooperative, for example, must be concerned about his business and clientele,[64] and Socialist politicians are too often concerned with electoral victory merely for its own sake.

Capitalism, for all this, has failed in Britain. Cole traces the arrival of Marxism (and Marx himself) in Britain and surmises that Marxism could not succeed in the face of Britain's advanced industrial development. Capitalism had prospered to the point at which enough workers were sharing in its benefits. This had clearly not been the case on the Continent. Subsequent events, and particularly the Great Depression of 1929, had shown that Socialism, including Marxism, still had great vitality and validity and that capitalism, by its very character, contained the seeds of its own destruction. Unlike Marx, Cole is not willing to accord an inevitability to Socialism; capitalism has often proved too resilient for that. He believes that the prospects for Socialism should be viewed as ever-improving and he bases this upon the hard fact of Britain's declining position in world trade, a position he expects to see steadily worsening over the next few decades. In this speculation he has been amply proved right.[65]

Cole's examination and description of capitalism in Britain includes a comment that "the trust. . .is still the exception in Great Britain."[66] A few firms, such as Unilever, Imperial Chemical Industries, and Coats Sewing Cotton fit this definition, but most firms and industries are characterized by an inability to establish monopolistic control of pricing and output.[67] Cole later developed a different view of the extent of monopoly capital, but this helps to explain a passage in *Self-Government in Industry* in which he excoriates those who insist upon antitrust action as a remedy for capitalism.[68] Antitrust action not only fails to get to the heart of the problem, but it *cannot* do this since it is a palliative action which applies to only a small section of business and industry. Cole might well have a sense of urgency about this today, since monopoly has become much more advanced in Britain and throughout the Western world through the device of multi-national corporate conglomerates which are answerable to no one.

A high level of worthwhile generalization is achieved in the section on the debate between Marxists and utopians. Cole clearly sides with the utopians as he takes issue with the three elements which make up the blend he calls the "Marxist gospel":

It is satisfying to feel right and rational; it is satisfying to feel strong; and it is satisfying to feel predestined to victory. . . . This doctrine may be believed because it is comforting; but it fails to comfort unless it is believed.[69]

Such a view also involves a fatal mistake, when it is applied to Britain, of placing all members of society into one of two classes.

The complexity of both the industrial system and the class system militate against this lack of realism.[70] Cole therefore takes the position, in *The Simple Case for Socialism* as in *Self-Government in Industry* and *Guild Socialism Restated*, that although there is no Utopia and that this is not in fact achievable, there is also no historical inevitability of Socialism, and Socialists must therefore place their faith in reason.[71] Marxists also place their faith in reason for they, like Cole, are not untouched by the Age of Enlightenment, but reason for them is reinforced by dynamics and processes emanating from class structure, industrial development, and history. Cole takes aim at the exclusivity of Marxism, which he alleges is rooted in these reinforcements and which makes the working and oppressed classes an "elect" group. Socialism is for everyone, states Cole, not just for an "elect," and he stresses the analogy to Calvinist predestination.[72] Cole also disagrees with the analysis of Fascism which some Marxists put forth in the early 1930s: that it was a passing phase between capitalism and Socialism in which the latter would be triumphant because of the excesses and the great amount of overt oppression brought by this phase. The cry of "After Hitler, us!" is for Cole too cynical, too unfeeling in the light of the great human suffering wrought by Fascism, and wholly incorrect in its assumptions.[73] Again Cole has been proved right by subsequent events, though his insight on this matter is neither remarkable nor unique.

The section on Marxism and utopianism is some of Cole's finest writing, but *The Simple Case* is also a good ready reference for Cole's oft-stated opposition to titles, monarchy, artificial class distinctions, and privilege. This is a more complex matter than it may at first seem to be, and the various charts, examinations, and explanations of the nuances of British class structure he provides illustrate the point well. A foremost goal of this analysis is to seek ways of winning over intermediate-class supporters for Socialism and to promote this through an understanding of the interrelationship of class and the state in Britain.[74] The monarchy, the apex of the class system, is incompatible with the development of a Socialist state. "Socialism is quintessentially republican" and the very presence of the monarchy is a manifestation of inequality, unearned income, and privilege.[75] Monarchy is difficult to combat since it is derived from an illegitimacy that few seek to question, and it is even the case that "monarchy" thrives in republics because of the widespread belief in the state for its own sake.[76] Cole wants to demystify the state, but his problem is an acute one since the state is usually taken as a "given" in any analysis of politics and society. The British state, with its trappings of pomp and majesty surrounding a venerated monarchy, continues to thrive upon traditions and customs rooted in prejudice and inequality. The enduring strength of the monarchy and the state for which it provided "legitimacy" during all of Cole's time and through today attests to the difficulty of Cole's position.

The House of Lords is also ripe for abolition, according to Cole, because it stands upon the same ground of illegitimacy, privilege, inequality, and uselessness.[77] The Lords is almost the epitome of the kind of institution Cole believes can be eliminated because of its functionless character. It serves only as a needless embellishment of the antiquated nature of British government, though it provides some difficulty on a few occasions for the operation of government and could presumably hamper a Socialist government for a short time.[78]

The House of Commons, for that matter, is a bulky and even burdensome device for the achievement of Socialism. It has been shown how Guild Socialist theory is ever suspect of conventional parliamentary institutions and critical of any claim that they are representative; but beyond this, the House of Commons is simply too slow and too inefficient for the enactment of measures that are Socialist or which can lead to a Socialist society.[79] Cole's criticism of the Commons on this score is borne out by the more conventional Socialists of the collectivist kind in their experiences of the 1945–1951 Labour government period, when they had to resort to "the guillotine" on debate and other methods in order to achieve passage of basic welfare–state measures which were to serve as what they perceived to be the foundation of a Socialist society.[80] The Commons' geographic base, as pointed out in the discussion of *Self-Government in Industry,* also renders it quite meaningless as a representative institution.

Planning is part and parcel of bringing change into government to fit Socialist needs, Cole believes, and this view—not remarkable today—is based on the sensible proposition that things simply cannot be allowed to drift. He advocates a National Plan, along the lines developed in the Soviet Union, as a necessary part of the government and of the economy and, even to one as antibureaucratic and anarchic as Cole, there is recognition of a need for full-time planners.[81] In connection with this position it is interesting to point out an associated idea which Cole did *not* opt for: the Trotskyist and later Maoist belief in "permanent revolution," which draws its sustenance in part from the willingness of bureaucrats, managers, educators, and others in the more privileged positions to work at menial tasks in industry and agriculture from time to time. It may at first seem strange that this did not occur to Cole, whose outlook and sensibilities demonstrated awareness of the stultifying effects with which a spirit of bureaucracy can pervade a government or society; but more than likely, the middle class and sometimes aristocratic Cole would have put aside "permanent revolution" as some sort of aberration.

Cole, like nearly all great political thinkers from the Greeks through Rousseau and beyond, was concerned with education and culture and the relationship of these to society. The reform of education is a major concern of *The Simple Case for Socialism,* which is not surprising in a work devoted to the ethical basis of Socialism. The British educational system is the specific object of his criticism in this section of the book. It is a system which fails because its basic premise fails: that education and culture are attainable only by certain people in certain social and economic classes. Cole denies this, asserting that their attainment by the working class or by anyone else is fully possible, and it is certain that he draws upon his experience in the workers' education movement as well as his common sense as he writes this.[82]

Much of the malaise in British education, like so many other things, can be laid to religious differences. Cole delineates the battle between "church and chapel"—the Church of England and the Nonconformists—over education, access to it, what doctrines should be taught, and what purposes education should serve.[83] The result is one of the most confusing systems of education in the world, one that is seldom understood by, or even explainable to, Britishers. The main characteristic of the system, however, is unmistakable: it is essentially two systems, one for the rich and one for the poor, with the latter placed at a severe disadvantage.[84] Such a system is not in accord with the principles of Socialism, for "a classless society demands a classless education."[85] It cannot be geared to scullery maids on the one hand and to Empire-builders on the other. Much of the rationale behind this pernicious bifurcation is connected with the idea that education is merely vocational. This is not the purpose of education, says Cole. Education is not something to be enjoyed or to be used to instill class values for one group while it is denied by the vocational emphasis and early school-leaving age visited upon another. Education is for all until a school-leaving age of eighteen.[86] Britain has yet to achieve this goal, but strides are being made toward some of the other goals Cole considered axiomatic for a sound education system in Britain: an abolition of sex discrimination, an opportunity to advance through merit rather than through class or connections (this now pervades the system), and the development of schools along "comprehensive" lines, incorporating the features both of grammar schools and of vocational education.[87] Cole's critique of education extends beyond the secondary level, and he asserts his belief that university education should be developed in all the larger cities and towns so that students will not be required to live away from home. He also blasts the inwardness and monasticism of Oxford and Cambridge, finding them to be at odds with the modern demands of society as well as with egalitarian principles.[88] Cole should receive special commendation for perceiving this, since his life was strongly affected by this kind of environment, and this was an environment he had often enjoyed and strongly cherished.

   The Simple Case for Socialism is a succinct and brilliant treatise. Cole developed a thorough and clearly reasoned line of argument for his case, and it is appreciated all the more when the dispiriting time in which it was written is recalled. No other work, except for the *History of Socialist Thought*, reveals the depth of Cole's Socialist faith so fully. Equally as important, however, is the contribution Cole has made to what could only be called "popular sociology." *The Simple Case for Socialism* stands as the best achievement in this genre until the appearance, three decades later, of Anthony Sampson's *Anatomy of Britain Today*. It mirrors and describes Britain of the 1930s so well that the reader can occasionally wander from the major purpose of the book into its richness of detail and insight. It also continues to be timely, since most of the institutions and policies which drew Cole's fire—economic inequality, vested privilege, the monarchy and the Lords, the bifurcated education system—remain in place and in force. The legitimacy of these, however, continues to be in doubt, and Cole did more than his share in promoting this doubt.

IV   The Meaning of Marxism

No Socialist can ignore Marx, and this is particularly true in Cole's case since he was a political theorist. Cole's heritage is linked with William Morris and Robert Owen more than it ever could be with Marx, but his strong admiration of the Marxist movement which had been brought to Britain in the nineteenth century, his catholicity and antisectarianism within the Socialist movement, and the fact that his chief source of inspiration, William Morris, was profoundly influenced by Marx in eschewing any form of "gradualism," are all important considerations in explaining Cole's interest in Marx.

Cole's views on Marx and Marxism provide as much insight about his thought processes and outlook as they do about the phenomena they seek to describe. Scholars of Marx and Marxism are often disdainful of *The Meaning of Marxism,* and it is claimed with some justification that Cole made an English Realist out of Marx.[89] Based largely upon a 1934 effort entitled *What Marx Really Meant,* this work has enjoyed a modest success; but no scholar of Cole would consider it his finest achievement and most would place it well below this standard.[90] Cole himself would not proclaim it as any kind of definitive guide to Marxism, and other writings of his own on the same subject—such as the analysis of influences upon Marx's thought in the *History of Socialist Thought*—are of greater value to students of Marxism.[91] *The Meaning of Marxism* is nonetheless uniquely valuable, for it reflects the thoughts of an English Guild Socialist upon the contributions and deficiencies of Marxism, and this is a topic of signal importance to any Socialist movement or thinker.

At the outset Cole states emphatically that he is not a Marxist.[92] He opposes not only Marx's system, with its foundations of Hegelianism and economic determinism, but any systems approach.[93] Systems approaches seek to account for too many diverse phenomena and they tend to preordain thought on any variances or events that may arise. This is the crux of Cole's criticisms of Marxism: it has been made into a dogma by its adherents, lessening the possibilities for critical thought and analysis. Marxism is taken by some to be holy writ, and this gives

such adherents a chance to explain everything in the name of
Marxism; though it is only Marxist fanatics of the worst kind who
learn in detail the writings in *Das Kapital*, the *Communist
Manifesto*, or say, the critique of the Gotha Program.[94] (Cole
could have added that this is also an activity of anti-Marxist
fanatics of the worst kind.)

   Cole is "Marx-influenced" all the same, and he acknowledges
the substantial debt that Guild Socialists, and nearly all other
Socialists, owe to Marx.[95] His main quibble with Marx is not with
the essential message of the need for Socialism or with most of
Marx's conclusions. It is with Marx's method.[96] This gives rise to a
peculiarity of Cole's thought, not commented upon heretofore
and not unusual among Anglo-Saxon thinkers: the logical and
methodical use of such dichotomous categories of thought. Cole
agrees with Marx and the Marxists on their conclusions but not on
their methods, he agrees with their ends but not with their
means, and he applauds certain results—the Russian Revolution
is an obvious example—while deploring, or at least opposing,
actions taken to achieve such results. There are immense
philosophical problems involved in arriving at such distinctions
as method and objective or ends and means. The validity of such
distinctions is highly questionable and is rejected out of hand by
a number of social scientists, by philosophers of science, and
even by activists dedicated to social and political change.[97] The
problem indeed goes beyond philosophy, logic, or social–science
methodology; and for a disciple of William Morris who owes a
great deal to that aesthetic tradition and utopian influence, it
may well be considered a flaw.

   Whether it is or not, Cole's critique of Marx's method is an
exercise in questioning and damning almost the entire gamut of
Marx's premises. Marx's economic determinism is not made
legitimate merely by his choice of the economic factor as the
"independent variable" by which all other social and political
phenomena are to be judged, measured, and explained any more
than, say, Max Weber's choice of the Protestant Ethic can serve
as a basis for assessing the social and political traditions of
Western countries.[98] Further, Marxist thought is not "science," as
it is claimed to be, for it does not subject itself to critical testing
of its claims and because, by seeking to explain everything, it
explains nothing. Rather than being a science, it is merely a
mélange of flat assertions.[99] Marxism posits a belief in progress

and, to a very substantial degree, in technological innovation and liberation, an idea it holds in common with the capitalists. Enough has been said of how this rankles Guild Socialist sensibilities so that nothing needs to be added except to note that Cole does not fail to miss this point and to level it with his best ammunition.[100]

The materialistic conception of history is given substantial treatment—more than can be covered here without referring the reader to the work itself; but one or two observations should be made. Cole puts particular emphasis upon the materialist conception as set out in the *Communist Manifesto*. This may be fair enough, since even though it was a political tract written for its times, it has been declared an "historical document" by Friedrich Engels, its coauthor, "which we no longer have any right to alter."[101] It is hardly the place to look for a definitive presentation of economic determinism by Marx, however; and the *Manifesto* states that this is not its purpose when it lists its foremost concern as the property question.[102] Cole uses what he feels is an obvious example, the rise of Fascism in Europe prior to World War II, to prove his point that the factors of the economy and of production cannot be considered the sole factors of social change. Fascism is held to be not a mere extension of capitalism, but a system unto itself brought into existence surely by economic factors but also by factors such as agrarian values and racism.[103] This argument, hardly conclusive to Marxists, is accompanied by a general agreement with Marx's case on the contradictions of capitalism and with his belief in the superiority of capitalism to feudal arrangements;[104] but again Cole places no importance upon the flow or evolution of history, and again Cole sets out his differences on the question of methodological, rather than substantive, grounds.

Cole also attacks the Marxian theory of "class." Some of his nitpicking on questions related to this and to "class conscious-ness" appear needless, self-evident, or merely tedious, but the thrust of the argument is that Marx has again chosen an independent variable almost at random and has ascribed a unity of thought and action to classes which is at best misleading and is at worst simply not in accord with the facts.[105]

There are some Marxists who cannot see a flapper use her lipstick without producing pat an explanation of her conduct in terms of the

powers of production and the class struggle. It is, of course, undeniable
that the prevalence of lipstick at a price within the normal flapper's
purse is a by-product of capitalist mass production, and has therefore
an economic cause; but in relation to world history it is a phenomenon
completely without significance, and also quite irrelevant to the class
struggle, as Marx would have been the first to agree. [106]

Not all Marxists are guilty of such dogmatism, but there has
nevertheless been this tendency from time to time within Marxist
movements, and the worst enemies of Marxism are its dogmatists.
They are "more Marxist than Marx," says Cole, and they
vulgarize every aspect of Marxist thought, from the theory of
value and surplus value to the questions of class consciousness or
the importance of the dialectic.[107] None of this can possibly be
worthwhile. The dialectic, for example, cannot be made into a
dogma; dialectical thinking can be a helpful aid to one's thought
processes, according to Cole, and he uses this tool himself. But
this is all it is: a tool for thinking, and nothing more.[108]
    The real value of this book is that it explains as much about
Cole as it does about Marx and the Marxists. It reveals how he
thinks, but it also exhibits his reaction to Socialist revolutionary
thought. He questions whether the bourgeois state must be
smashed, and he goes on to state why it is possible to enact
Socialism through constitutional and parliamentary means.[109]
This is consistent with Cole's position in his other works, but
what is remarkable is the great degree of optimism he displays
about parliamentary and constitutional processes. He has seldom
gone to such lengths to demonstrate an almost complete faith in
the capture of the state machinery by Socialists.[110]
    The Meaning of Marxism has two other distracting features.
The first is that although Cole is quite clear in making
distinctions between Marx and Marxists, he makes no distinctions
between Marxist philosophy set out at one time in the great
theoretician's life from another, and these distinctions—when
one considers the young Marx, for example—are important. The
other is that Cole wrestles inordinately with the problem of the
increasing embourgeoisement of the working class, a matter of
considerable concern during the last two or three decades of his
lifetime. Recent research has shown that this is less of a problem
than it once seemed to be, and this is particularly the case in

British society. This makes the question less relevant and, to some degree, less interesting.[111]

The fundamental issues between Cole and the Marxists are clearly evident throughout the book. They consist, in sum, of Cole's great reluctance to resort to extralegal or revolutionary methods in order to achieve Socialism, of Cole's antisystems outlook, his antitechnology bias, his rejection of Hegelian philosophy and of most uses of the dialectic, his objection to the idea of the working class as the exclusive vehicle for the achievement of Socialism, and his rather typically Anglo-Saxon insistence upon such distinctions as method and objective, ends and means, and process and dogma. The consideration of method is most important in explaining these differences, for the processes of abstraction, conceptualization, and testing as they occurred in Cole's mind appear to be far different in essence than they were in the case of Marx and his various Continental followers and inheritors.

V A History of Socialist Thought

G. D. H. Cole's last literary project was the five-volume, seven-book effort of monumental proportions which he entitled *A History of Socialist Thought*. Its title is slightly misleading; it goes much farther than these boundaries and becomes in fact a history of Socialist movements as well. This apparently was not the original intention of Cole, for he believed that such a task was well-nigh impossible for a single author, and writing a history of thought would permit him to set some limits to a seemingly endless endeavor. He has nonetheless done the impossible, and his work is considered an "immense achievement, never before attempted by any scholar of any country."[112] It is acclaimed as "the fullest history of modern Socialism ever written in any language, an encylopaedia of the international Socialist movement. . . ."[113]

Clearly this is an even greater accomplishment when one considers that Cole was in exceedingly poor health during the last decade of his life. A tremendous amount of energy and willpower would be required to complete it. Cole recognized this himself, since he speculated about his ability to complete the work in his introduction to the penultimate volume.[114] Completion of *A History of Socialist Thought* must therefore be recognized as one of his foremost goals in the declining years of his life, and the credit due to him for nearly finishing it is almost as great as the credit for the work itself. He in fact did not quite complete the last volume, according to Margaret Cole, for she had to scrap one unrevised chapter and rewrite another.

This is more than a history; it is a great, comparative, political-and social-science project which employed experts in Socialist studies from many societies. It is a symbolic effort as well, signifying Cole's late-found conversion to internationalism and his belief that Socialism can only be achieved through the development of a worldwide movement which owed very little to the rather bourgeois Socialist and Social Democratic parties of various countries.

The always modest and self-effacing Cole is evident in every major part of this history, even to the point of making it slightly inaccurate. A reader of the section on Guild Socialism could not become immediately aware of Cole's significant contributions in this area of Socialist thought, though presumably this could be done by following up on the footnotes and bibliography. For the less diligent, it would be impossible to know that

for a few stormy months at the end of the [First World] war he (Cole) had wielded so much influence within the trade unions that he was talked about as a possible leader of a British revolution.[115]

Adherence to the Guild Socialist viewpoint is quite another matter. Cole clearly sets out, in his introduction to the fourth volume, his belief in the uniqueness and importance of Guild Socialism despite its lack of acceptance on a scale comparable to Communism or to orthodox Social Democracy.[116]

Cole's great humility is further exhibited in an unnecessary passage which appears at the outset of his work on the first volume:

Even within the more modest limits on what I am attempting I am very conscious of my shortcomings. I have no Russian, almost no Spanish, very little Italian, and not much German; and I hate reading German, and avoid it whenever I can. I tend therefore to use English or French translations of works in these languages where they exist, and to refer to German originals of translated works only when I want to be sure a passage has not been wrongly rendered.[117]

This rather amazing apology is more or less repeated at the outset of the second volume. Cole's mastery of great volumes of complex subject matter, so obvious throughout this history, underscores the needlessness of such apologies; but that is Cole's way, and it fully conforms with his character.

There is a heavy emphasis upon biography throughout the five volumes, which should not be surprising in the light of Cole's interest in people and of his biographies of Owen, Cobbett, Morris, Hardie, and others. This tendency is noticeable in the first volume, *The Forerunners, 1789–1850*, which deals with Socialism prior to its support by mass movements, a time of the ideals of such men as Saint-Simon, Owen, and Fourier. *A History of Socialist Thought* really begins with Saint-Simon and with the French Revolution, although Cole duly notes the earlier contributions of Thomas More's *Utopia* and other works. The first volume also contains excellent descriptive and analytical work on *The Communist Manifesto*.[118]

Volume Two is *Marxism and Anarchism, 1850=1890*. Unlike the first volume, which deals with a vast array of theorists and movements, this one deals with the growth of international Socialism as a movement and with the more or less clear-cut clash between the Marxists and the Anarchists. This period is paralleled by the growth and importance of trade unions, which had a significant impact on the development of Socialist ideology. Volume Two deals with Socialism in a variety of national settings, but the development of Socialism as an international movement becomes a consistent theme which must be considered the primary emphasis of the *History*. Cole is forced by the exigencies of his chronological approach to drop this subject from time to time, but he always returns to it and the narrative eventually blends national and international considerations reasonably well.

In this second volume, Cole also first gives significant space to American Socialism and the American labor movement. He traces the origins of these movements and develops the first of his several critiques on the failure of Socialism in America and on the peculiar role and attitude of the American labor movement, particularly the AFL, within the international labor movement.

Not surprisingly, and with ample justification, he devotes an entire chapter to William Morris and the late-nineteenth-century revival of British Socialism, but he does not permit his strong views of support for Morris to interfere with a quite objective narrative.

The Second International, 1889–1914, is the third volume. It is primarily concerned with the debates between revolutionary and Bernsteinist, or parliamentary, Socialists. The 1905 Russian Revolution also receives considerable attention, as one would expect, and Cole documents the proliferation of Socialist consciousness throughout the world. It is fair to say that Cole's *History* is Europe-centered until he proceeds to this volume, but this is simply because Socialist thought was also Europe-centered. The all-embracing, encylopedic, and internationalist character of the *History* is manifested in the sections on such widely scattered and disparate societies as Mexico, New Zealand, Australia, South Africa, China, Japan, Belgium, Spain, Scandinavia, and the Balkan countries.

Cole displays great respect for the genius of Rosa Luxemburg, Socialist theoretician and leader of the cause in Poland, Russia, Germany, and other Central and Eastern European countries. He notes her contributions to internationalism—she was one of the truly international leaders of Socialism in the decades before and after the turn of the century—and to Socialist economics. Most important were her theoretical contributions on political organization, particularly her prophetic insistence upon democratically organized mass parties committed to Socialism.[119] This was one of her major differences with Lenin, who insisted upon cadre-based party organization and a system of centralized party control. Cole and most Western Socialist observers believe that this debate and its resolution in favor of Lenin was a fateful development which ultimately led to the Socialist-Communist split which Cole repeatedly and urgently abhors. Lenin's major advantage, of course, lay in the fact that his revolutionary movement succeeded, and even in the Socialist world there is nothing which succeeds more than success. Rosa Luxemburg's only solace, in retrospect and in the view of Cole, is that she has been proved right, though she did not live to see these turns of events. Her approach to Socialism was of course far different from that of Cole, and they cannot be effectively compared because of the great differences in their respective environments. She was a revolutionary in every sense, but she shares with Cole the distinctions of being a Socialist who always insisted upon a democratized party structure and of looking beyond sectarianism to the broad areas of agreement which could potentially unite Socialists of every country. Cole strongly appreciates this.

The third volume also contains a critique on Georges Sorel, which is of compelling interest since this Syndicalist leader and theoretician must be considered a distant ideological relative of any Guild Socialist. Cole dislikes Sorel. They are both antirational, but Sorel is to a much greater degree. Sorel is "quite impossible to pin down except in negative terms."[120] He did not believe in democracy or in progress, or in the validity of reason as a basis for action. He eschewed any supposed value of trying to conciliate differences, and, according to Cole, he was much more against the bourgeoisie than for the workers. In addition, Sorel enjoyed the contradictions of life and saw no reason to attempt a resolution of them. Cole lived with ambiguity, but he never enjoyed it and was always uncomfortable with it.[121] Sorel's insistence upon violent and heroic revolution was, however, the most regrettable side of his thought from Cole's point of view:

> The reader will have perceived some time ago that I acutely dislike Sorel as a thinker, though I have a great deal of sympathy for the Syndicalism which for a time he espoused. It may be, on occasion, necessary to fight, and cowardice not to; but fighting is always, at best, a necessary evil, and there is nothing ennobling about it. Quite the contrary. It is perfectly possible to admire initiative, elan and determination without falling into the evil position of admiring combativeness in its own right. It is also . . . possible to accept "contradictions" . . . without regarding each "contradiction" as the occasion for a struggle leading to mutual extermination, in the Hegelian manner, or as an opportunity for the purposeless exercise of heroic virtues, as I think Sorel, despite all his "moralism," came in effect to do.[122]

Cole points out, by way of contrast, that Bill Haywood, the American leader of the IWW, believed that he was going somewhere toward a realizable objective, even though he, like Sorel, was an Anarcho-Syndicalist. Sorel was regarded by Cole as a mere pessimist "moaning for blood."[123]

The third and fourth volumes span two books each. The latter, entitled *Communism and Social Democracy, 1914=1931*, covers the Russian Revolutions of 1917, the German Revolution and Counterrevolution of 1918-1921, the General Strike in Britain,

104

the factors leading to the rise of Fascism in Italy, and the great
despond which affected Socialists of all countries during and
after World War I. It also describes the founding of the
International Labour Organization and the beginnings of the
Third, or Communist, International (Comintern) and the rivalry
of the Second and Third International movements during the
1920s. The breadth of the fourth volume, like the third, is very
great, and there are chapters on Socialism in China, Canada,
Latin America, India, the Antipodes, and other countries.

The October Revolution in Russia in 1917 overshadows all
other considerations in this fourth volume; indeed, says Cole, it is
the most important event since the French Revolution not only
for Socialism, but for the history of the world.[124] The Introduction sets out the many reasons why Socialist attitudes toward the
Soviet Union have been ambivalent: at first it was a matter of joy
and encouragement to nearly all Socialists, and later there were
sharp divisions over the nature, characteristics, faults, and
achievements of the regime. The focus of the debate centered
upon Lenin's conception of "democratic centralism" and upon
the idea of the "dictatorship of the proletariat." Cole is
convinced that these principles, originating (as far as Soviet
leaders are concerned) with Lenin and not with Stalin, laid the
groundwork for Stalinism.[125] Cole is strongly critical of the Soviet
Union most of the time in his Introduction, and he is particularly
critical of Stalin and his gross errors, but he nowhere conceded
the possibility in this *History* that Stalin represents an aberration
within the Communist movement which led to betrayal of the
principles of the Revolution. He is also critical of Stalin's
nationalism, which was a far more important force for the Soviet
dictator than his Communism, and of his promotion of the idea of
"Socialism in one country"—the belief that the welfare of the
Soviet state must take priority over the consideration of
revolutions for other countries.[126] It is rather odd, in the light of
this, that Cole takes such a dim view of Leon Trotsky and the
Trotskyist, or Fourth International, movement, which led the
fight against "Socialism in one country" and against the
subsequent excesses and terrorism engendered by Stalinism.
Cole gives the reader no explanation for this, nor, more
surprisingly, does he attempt to capture the general Western and
capitalist attitude of great relief after the so-called "moderate"
and "pragmatic" Stalin had prevailed over the "doctrinaire"

Trotsky.[127] The only plausible explanation for this is that the Trotskyists, like all Communists, are also revolutionaries, for another passage, written in a separate context for the fifth volume, refers to the international Trotskyist movement as a "nuisance group."[128]

Cole continues, in this fourth volume, to thread his way through the tortuous story of the rival international Socialist and trade-union movements. He neither aligns himself with the Second International nor with the Communists, but states his preference for the Centre Group of the Vienna Union, a comparatively small and shortlived organization devoted to bridging the gap between the two great rivals.[129] Cole also carries on his narrative on the American labor movement and its relationship to international trade unionism. The firm anti-Socialism of Samuel Gompers prevented even a modicum of cooperation between the AFL and the Social Democratic unions of Western Europe, and this established a tradition which extends to the present day, for it has affected George Meany and the AFL-CIO so much that, by and large, American labor is outside the mainstream of international trade unionism.

The fifth volume, *Socialism and Fascism, 1931-1939,* was published posthumously. Cole used 1939 as a rough "cut-off" date, though he wrote of some events up through 1945 and even beyond. The choice of date, though arbitrary as such choices invariably are, was based upon Cole's belief that subsequent events had been too recent for accurate historical interpretation. This last volume deals primarily with the economic collapse which characterized the period leading to World War II, but also devotes considerable space to the Spanish Civil War, the development of Communism in China, the Blum "Popular Front" in France, the AFL-CIO split in America, and the Soviet Union from the beginning of the First Five Year Plan in 1928. Volume Five was originally planned to include chapters on India and Israel as well, but the death of Cole, and the editing problems of Margaret Cole and Julius Braunthal in putting the volume together, ruled these out.

Chapter 13 of this fifth volume, entitled "Looking Backwards and Forewards"—he had Edward Bellamy in mind—must be looked upon as Cole's final testament and his final measurement of the place of Socialism in the world. Again he takes a broad, internationalist view, and again he emphasizes the common

Marxist basis of both Socialist and Communist movements. He again demonstrates his acute awareness of the great gap between Soviet Communists and Western Socialists, and he feels that this is a grievous situation—he calls it a "calamitous gulf"— but he assigns much of the responsibility for it to the antilibertarian nature of the Soviet regime which, in turn, he believes has emanated from the traditions of Russian political culture.[130]

The five volumes contain some remarkable observations on lesser-known Socialist movements and leaders. A good example of this is Cole's appreciation of the importance of Antonio Gramsci, the Italian leader and theorist who established innovations in guidance and tactics for the Italian Communist party. This recognition of Gramsci occurs well before many of his works have been translated or have become known internationally.[131] Unfortunately, Cole's coverage of Tito and Yugoslavia does not proceed far enough chronologically to include any analysis of Yugoslav experiments in workers' control, a matter in which he held a keen interest.

How can one develop a broad criticism of *A History of Socialist Thought*? How can a critique be derived which has any meaning that is independent of the overwhelming contribution made by this work? This is not impossible for some individuals: some Marxists have indicated, for example, that they believe it has major faults.[132] These tend to be grounded in ideological interpretation, however, and they cannot detract from the great amount of research and effort which went into this *History* nor from the landmark nature of Cole's contribution. The truth of the matter is that the *History* is difficult to criticize because there is nothing that is comparable. It is, as Julius Braunthal points out, "a monumental work [which] will remain the standard work on the history of Socialism for many years to come."[133]

VI *Other Major Works*

Workshop Organisation deserves special mention as an important piece of historical analysis by Cole. Written in 1923, it details the growth of the shop stewards' movement in Britain, a movement which was always close, in terms of ideology and purpose, to Cole, and which looked upon him as its most important intellectual leader and theorist. *Workshop Organisation* has been reissued in a new edition.[134] *A Century of Cooperation* is dedicated to another cause close to Cole's heart and interests, and it is probably one of the best works in the field. This history performs much the same service for the cooperative movement that *Workshop Organisation* does for the shop stewards.[135] *Studies in Class Structure* has received considerable acclaim from sociologists. Although it is a dry document in a number of places, it updates some of the work on British social classes, including the titled ones, which appeared in *The Simple Case for Socialism*. It also forms part of a continuum with such later efforts as W. L. Guttsman's *The British Political Elite* and is an important part of the bibliographies on British elites and class structure. The effectiveness of *Studies in Class Structure* is also greatly enhanced by an introductory section in which Cole grapples with the difficult relationship between class structure and the impact of technology.[136] *The World of Labour* holds a special place as Cole's first book and as a turning point toward his road to Guild Socialism. Like other well-known Cole works, it has been reissued in a new edition.[137] Another interesting period piece is *The People's Front*, an antiwar tract of 1937 written for the Left Book Club, which calls for Socialist-Communist cooperation in the anti-Fascist and anti-Nazi cause. Probably no other Cole work was so overtaken by events as this one. The Hitler–Stalin Pact crushed the feasibility of any such approach, and *The People's Front* demonstrates well that Cole was as capable as anyone else in misreading trends and events.[138] *Economic Tracts for the Times* is almost never listed among Cole's major works, but it is a good descriptive social window on the early 1930s and it contains kernels of Cole's thought on Socialism that are both important and unobtainable elsewhere.[139] *Socialist Economics* would not be recognized by many economists as a part of their discipline at all. It posits a familiar list of Cole themes of 1950, and it contains surprisingly little of his Guild Socialist outlook. It emphasizes the humaneness of Socialism, welcomes the rise of Keynesian economics and the Welfare State, though it does not regard these as substitutes, and talks about such concerns as planning and income distribution. This is one of the most Fabian works Cole ever produced, and the quality of the writing suffers a bit because of it.[140] *Essays in Social Theory* is, as one could guess from the title, a miscellany, but it is most valuable for Cole's interpretations of a variety of thinkers and events which have been significant in the development of Western political thought—Rosseau, Comte, the Victorian Age, the Communist Manifesto, and the evolution of social science in the twentieth century. Rather unique insights into Cole's thinking can also be gleaned from choice nuggets on the teaching of social science, on the philosophy of education, on the essentials of democracy, and on the rights of humanity. The *Essays* are brilliant little pieces.[141] Cole's many short histories— of working-class movements, trade unions, cooperatives, and "common people"—are also significant, along with the hundreds of pamphlets, reviews, monographs, and articles, but one article, "Thoughts After the Election," which appeared in the *New Statesman* in 1955, is particularly indicative of both the national and international views on Socialism held by Cole at this late point in his life.[142]

CHAPTER 5

Cole's Legacy

DISTINGUISHED scholars and political leaders around the world—Mr. Kofe Busia of Ghana, Professor Stephen Bailey of the United States, Mr. David Lewis of Canada, Dr. Jim Cairns of Australia, and Mr. Eric Heffer of Britain are good examples— have attested to the influence and character of G. D. H. Cole. These of course are direct contacts and personal acquaintances, but the importance of each of these examples is indicative of the exponential growth of Cole's influence and ideas. At the less direct level, it can be shown that Cole's histories, textbooks, theoretical works, and political philosophy place him in a strong position alongside such contemporaries as R. H. Tawney, Harold Laski, Bertrand Russell, and the Webbs, and his contributions and achievements may outlast all of these.

Cole's legacies and influences are as varied as they are profound, and it is therefore difficult to list or even suggest all of them. In writing, they range from detective fiction and lucid journalism to a precise and occasionally rarified science of politics, economics, and society. In activity, they range through the various roles he assumed at different times—social reformer, research organizer and administrator, political candidate, educational innovator, Labour spokesman, and political theorist. And his life-style, though badly handicapped by poor health, ranges from a position as an uncloistered don to one of an active and effective leader of the working class.

Influences which are not directly traceable must necessarily take on a tentative and indeed speculative character. It is important to realize that Socialism, including the democratic versions of it which have arisen in Britain, as well as small and decentralized government, and even workers' control, are all important political ideas and ideals which would have come into existence apart from any contribution to their development by

G. D. H. Cole. Bearing this in mind, it is still possible to set out, within such limits, the importance and relevance of Cole's legacy to a number of ideas and trends of twentieth-century political writing. In some areas the ability to trace the importance of Cole is easier than in others: in workers' control literature he is the preeminent writer of his age, but in other matters—the opposition of technocratic biases, for example—he is one of many writers and thinkers who have made significant contributions.

An incompleteness will nevertheless persist after most exercises of this kind are undertaken, and this is because Cole is an understudied subject. In part this stems from the sheer volume of his work, for he is one of the most prolific writers of all time. Equally important, however, is the fact that Cole wrote his books, pamphlets, and articles for contemporary audiences, and the impact of this, from the standpoint of anyone doing research on Cole, is that it is necessary to wade through great reams on the social, economic, and political concerns of 1925, 1938, or whenever, in order to find those choice kernels of his thought which make him a great figure.[1]

I   The Reshaping of Socialist Thought

The preceding chapters, and especially the discussion of *The Simple Case for Socialism*,[2] demonstrate his unique legacy to the reshaping of Socialist theory. No one who has had the slightest familiarity with Cole can logically assert or presume that Socialism in any form is tantamount to conditions of sprawling bureaucracy, to the apparatus of the Big State, or to Sovietized or collectivized tyranny. Certainly there remain political observers, politicians, and even an occasional scholar who equate Socialism with centralized structures, nationalization of industry, and a high degree of governmental planning. Von Mises and other critics of Cole have charged him or his Guild Socialism with these faults and shortcomings, but it is difficult for them to substantiate such a charge. In part this is because Guild Socialism has never really been tried; but its adherents, and especially Cole, eschew such ideas, and it is quite possible that the heavy ammunition leveled against centralization by Cole and like-minded Socialists amounts to a more effective argument against it than any which have emanated from Von Mises or other Rightists.[3]

Quite unlike any Marxists, who adhere on the one hand to a Soviet, Chinese, or a similar model or who, on the other, support some form of the Western or Bernsteinist model of democratic and nonrevolutionary Socialism, Cole sought to put Socialists in touch with much older—and, some would say, more valuable—utopian ideals and traditions of preindustrial civilization.[4] Marxists of almost any stripe have given short shrift to craftsmanship and job satisfaction, but to Cole these were of paramount importance. He grappled with technocracy and he adamantly defied the presumption in its favor which the Marxists were so willing to concede. A freethinker, he did not wish to see the spirit of obeisance to a traditional God merely replaced by deference to a Machine God. His antitechnological bias makes him appear prophetic in a world now faced with newly found concerns about blight, environment, alienation, conformity, plasticization, and oppression. Socialism cannot—in the light of Cole's ideals—be equated with the variety of misguided views of what constitutes progress, or with the desirability of economic growth without regard to its consequences, or with construction of public works projects merely for their own sake, or with the element of "mass" in mass society and mass culture.

Large-scale bureaucracy, according to Cole, brings most of these undesirable forces into being or, at the least, aids and abets their intrusion and their growth. This is why he wrote, at the end of his great *History of Socialist Thought:*

I am neither a Communist nor a Social Democrat, because I regard both as creeds of centralisation and bureaucracy, whereas I feel sure that a Socialist society that is to be true to its equalitarian principles of human brotherhood must rest on the widest possible diffusion of power and responsibility, so as to enlist the active participation of as many as possible of its citizens in the tasks of democratic self-government.[5]

There are clear indications, in the New Left and in other Socialist movements, that Socialist thought is moving in these directions, and while a direct measure of Cole's influence must remain uncertain, it is safe to say that he has helped to chart this new course.

II *Redirecting British Socialism*

The influence of Cole appears, upon first impression, to be less important when it is viewed against the theoretical and ideological development of British Socialism. There is no question that the "mainstream" of any specifically British kind of Socialism in the twentieth century has been collectivist, with heavy emphases upon nationalization, centralization, "good government" along practical lines as set out by the Webbs, subservience of trade unions to politicians and party leaders,[6] and strong, if often unstated, support for Parliament and for the British political system. Cole believed that all of this is marginally better than Toryism and that the alleviation of human suffering which the modern welfare state could bring about was very worthwhile, though he would not define this as Socialism. He believed nonetheless that it was all a terribly misguided attempt to solve the problems of society and that it was an unnecessarily complicated and vexing approach which did not seek out basic questions or answers.

On the other hand, it is rather difficult to detect the "mainstream" of nineteenth-century British Socialism, and Cole took lessons as well as comfort from some of the ideas of the Owenites, the Chartists, and the Hyndeman Marxists. British Socialism in the nineteenth century was both more utopian and less institutionalized than in the twentieth, which brought with it a variety of research institutes, hair-splitting groups, workers' education movements, Socialist societies, and the creation of the Labour party, with its conferences, MPs, and bureaucracy. The growth of bureaucracy is also characteristic of the trade unions and the cooperatives. Some of the twentieth-century groups— the National Guilds League, the New Fabian Research Bureau, and the Socialist Society for Information and Propaganda are examples—were anticollectivist in their orientation and purpose. But these were exceptions. The bulk of organized Socialist and affiliated groups in Britain in this century have come out of a Webbian mold. This is also the case with most of the literature on British Socialism. Cole and the Guild Socialists, as well as their like-minded legatees of the New Left, are probably of no more than third-place importance in the literature of British Socialism if sheer bulk is used as a criterion, for Webbian collectivist writers must be followed by a second category of specifically

Marxist writers who have produced many more reams of material than have the anticollectivists.

Cole, for all of this, has heavily influenced the course of British Socialism. His Guild movement lived on even after the formal death of the League in the mid-1920s. Its ideals were part and parcel of the SSIP and the New Fabian Research Bureau in the 1930s. Its proponents and heirs sought to influence, and in some ways did influence, the programs and policies of the 1945-51 Labour government. Less obvious in the 1950s except perhaps in Cole's writings, it burst upon the British political scene in a slightly, and only very slightly, altered form in the 1960s. One component of difference was semantical, though there is no question that New Left ideology contains Marxist as well as Guild dimensions. At the beginning of the 1970s, Guild Socialist principles, though they had been altered in form, had found a new strength and following in Britain and in the world, and the British trade-union movement and Labour party had incorporated the principles of workers' control into their statements and manifestoes for the first time.[7]

During all of this time Cole's writings have been influential and have manifested the continuing presence and significance of his ideas. He has therefore made a continuing contribution to the Guild Socialist and New Left causes, but it is just as important that he has inflicted doubts upon the minds of the less self-assured Big State Socialists and has tempered the hand of those who govern or seek to govern. Whether Cole has been in the "mainstream" of British Socialism is not terribly important, then, for he has surely affected the "mainstream" while performing a role as its most articulate opposition leader.

Less positive evidence of Cole's influence on British Socialism is the great and sometimes severe criticism to which his work was subjected all during his lifetime and even posthumously.[8] Such efforts, it is fair to say, are usually directed at influential thinkers.

A great deal of the redirection and reshaping of British Socialism which has occurred in this century and which appears bound to occur in the future can thus be traced to Cole's influence and, in addition, evidence appears to be mounting that the collectivist "mainstream" is increasingly a phenomenon of the past. Socialists and non-Socialists alike are seeking out new life-styles, new forms of social and political organization, new

approaches to problems, and new—and sometimes old—ways of
bringing humankind into more harmonious relationships with
nature and with one another. A Neo-Guild Socialism can
probably find a place in this panoply of concerns.

III   Workers' Control

Any attempt to measure or summarize Cole's influence leads
to the subject of workers' control. The significant and international dimensions of this renewed concern are increasingly
evident in the host of books, articles, and research papers
devoted to it, and many or most of these efforts cite Cole and his
work as singular and preeminent in performing historic roles of
innovation and theory-building. Cole's writings and findings have
reached a wide audience in those fields devoted to practical
experimentation and application—industrial sociology, industrial
management, social psychology, and industrial relations. His
preeminent positions as a writer, as chief proponent of Guild
Socialism, and as an originator of theory and planning for models
of industrial organization and governance all tend to make it
inevitable that his influence is both broad and deep. His
contributions to workers' control have been published in more
than a dozen languages, and experimentation based upon his
ideas has taken place well beyond the boundaries of Britain and
the English-speaking countries.

The work of Cole has served as an important reference point
in the development of the political and economic organization of
present-day Yugoslavia.[9] Yugoslavia considers itself to be a state
in which the principle of workers' control is operative, and much
of the rationale of the state centers upon the belief that an
essential form of democracy is carried out within this framework.

It is fitting, from a number of standpoints, that Cole played a
role of some influence and inspiration in Yugoslav development
and planning. The joining of theory and practice has always been
a hallmark of many of the great and creative political theorists—
Plato, Aristotle, Machiavelli, Rousseau, Marx. They were important to the politics of their respective times and places. The great
classical theorists wrote and compared constitutions.
Machiavelli, the first modern theorist, effectively brought
"politics" and "policy" together (which should not be too
surprising, since these terms are derived from the same root), but

he also compared and wrote about constitutional principles while offering up sage advice to the Borgias. Rousseau wrote a constitution for Corsica and served to inspire the French Revolution. And G. D. H. Cole, though he was not an author of any constitution for any state—a role which would have horrified his anarchistic sensibilities—has provided many of the theoretical underpinnings for one of the most interesting social and political experiments of this century. It is well established that Cole was important to British Socialism and therefore to British government as well, but his contribution to Yugoslav statecraft tends to underscore his transcendence across time and national borders.

It is also fitting because Yugoslavia was founded upon some of the concerns and emphases which typified Cole's work. The development of a workers' control system was a direct outgrowth of concern over the sprawling and unresponsive Yugoslav bureaucracy.[10] It is also connected with Yugoslavia's determination to chart its own path to Socialism, which grew out of Tito's much-publicized and courageous break with Stalin's great Soviet military and economic machine in 1948. This was a move which Cole greatly admired.[11]

Yugoslavia continues to be a great center of attention for scholars and political observers who are interested in workers' control. There is no question that this small Balkan country fails as an ideal laboratory, for its standard of what constitutes democracy does not meet Cole's specifications; but making allowances, as Cole did, it is possible to see that cultural diversity and frictions, the presence of the Soviet threat, economic considerations arising out of Yugoslavia's underdevelopment when compared to the West, and a welter of other considerations have prevented any possibility of emergence of anything resembling a Western-style democratic state. This is apparently also the case when considerations are narrowed to the question of *economic* democracy, though this is affected by questions of degree and nuance as well as those standard variables— consultation arrangements, decision-making levels, the role of managers, trade unions, the party organization, etc.—which are capable of of yielding a great variety of analyses. There are also the inevitable questions of comparability: how are "efficiency" and "production," for example, to be defined in a workers' control system?[12] These do not mean the same thing that they would mean in a profit-oriented capitalist enterprise.

The Yugoslav experiment is, all the same, producing some interesting studies and findings. Among them is one which asserts that it is possible, at least in a tentative fashion, to show that "efficiency" and "production," even when these are defined in a traditional American and capitalist framework, are found to be in existence at highly satisfactory levels within the Yugoslav economy and that this can be correlated with job satisfaction and with workers' control.[13] Another study asserts that the Yugoslav system could be adapted to the United States as a way of insuring the abolition of poverty.[14]

In any event, Yugoslavia represents only one model of workers' control. A variety of circumstances, goals, needs, legal arrangements, and political power alignments has yielded a number of models, and it is probable that a typology of these models will be developed.[15] Even the term "workers' control" is rejected by some scholars who feel that it is quite meaningless. They may prefer a term such as "self-management," which is less likely to conjure up images of class, political power, and political conflict. Cole's writings display a marked preference, however, for "workers' control," despite his rejection of a Marxist view of such terms. Semantical dimensions are important, as Cole realized, and his choice of term is rooted in his belief that control equals power and that workers' control is, both first and finally, a political question.[16]

Cole has had a strong influence on other models of workers' control. His works have served through most of this century as doctrinal guideposts for the British shop stewards' movement, which has been perennially critical of branch—rather than shop—organization of the unions, of union bureaucracy and centralization, and of the remoteness from the workers that too often characterizes such large entities as the Transport and General Workers Union, the Amalgamated Union of Engineering Workers, or the even more centralized federation, the British Trades Union Congress. The strong thread of Guild Socialism can be traced through the shop stewards' movement to the present day, and it surfaces in writings, periodicals, the unions, the TUC, the Labour party, and in industrial disputes.[17] Cole's works also have had a traceable influence upon workers' control movements, both large and small, in Canada, Australia, New Zealand, Scandinavia, and Continental Europe, but these movements have not had an effect upon their respective societies, generally speaking, that is comparable to the British experience.[18] He is at least a marginal influence on the Clydeside shipbuilding workers in Scotland, whose shop stewards led a successful workers' control movement after the demise of their capitalist employer. A similar workers' control experiment developed in the wake of the financial collapse of a motorcycle works in 1974.[19] A number of temporary takeovers of British industrial firms by the workers in recent years also signifies a growth in industrial support for the principle of workers' control.[20] All of these cases are demonstrations of workers' belief in themselves as both the directors and instruments of production, marketing, and administration, and all have involved emphases upon workers' rights, security, control, job satisfaction, and craftsmanship.

It remains clear, of course, that many of these models and examples are only partially influenced by G. D. H. Cole and Guild Socialism. In the case of Yugoslavia, for example, the fact that the entire economic planning apparatus is state-inspired and largely state-directed stands as an important deviation. The Clydeside shipbuilders were largely Communist-led, and a variety of influences, to say nothing of the grievances, caused industrial workers to resort to takeover actions in Britain in recent years.

It is not difficult to document the widespread emphasis upon job satisfaction that is characteristic of industrialized societies today. The maxim that a happy worker is also productive meets very few demurrers.[21] Cole's task of arguing this point was somewhat more onerous than would be the case today, but rhetoric and practice always diverge, especially in the case of big business, and dissatisfaction in the workplace has remained a problem of strikingly constant proportions over the past several decades. The popularity of Studs Terkel's best-seller *Working*, the attention given to job satisfaction in management-training institutes and in a variety of television documentaries, the emphasis upon, and demand for, grievance settlement—particularly at the local level—in labor-management negotiations, and the close connection between alienation in the workplace and social anomie are all indicative of public interest and concern with this question. Responses of capitalist enterprises are varied—mechanisms for consultation and for grievance procedures, a heavy dose of paternalism (Japan is perhaps the prime example here), an occasional bow in the direction of a worker voice in management,[22] or simply ignoring such matters.

In some instances there has been a partial recognition of the problem. Perhaps the most spectacular example in recent years has been the case of the Volvo firm in Sweden. Consultative and participatory machinery have been established for a worker role in production planning, assignment of tasks, and requisites of the work environment. These are of course the kinds of concerns Cole wrote about, but most importantly, there is recognition of the need of a sense of craftsmanship, and of the need to develop a closer proximity between the worker and the finished product. This idea, which is so central to Cole's writing and thinking and, before him, to William Morris and John Ruskin, is being revived in the face of the twentieth-century mass-production techniques, mass consumption, mass society, computerization, cost accounting, and indifference. It is a small but significanct piece of evidence that Cole's prescriptions for industrial life are not only relevant, but that they can be rediscovered in the presence of awesome obstacles.[23]

This must be a source of satisfaction to Cole's admirers and to those who find contemporaneity and trenchant purpose in his work.[24] Recognition of this need and the application of a remedy aimed at its fulfillment is indeed an occasion to be celebrated. This falls far short of what Cole would describe as workers' control, but so has almost everything else. At this point in time and at this stage of humanistic consciousness in industrial development, it may seem too exacting and almost absurd to begrudge the significance of such a landmark on the basis that this is not equivalent to industrial democracy;[25] but more to the point is the realization that mere recognition of the important place of craftsmanship does not insure an appreciation of the depth of alienation in late twentieth-century industrial life.

Cole's legacy to workers' control has remained preeminent for more than half a century because much of it is enactable, and, as previously noted, this is one of the few instances in the history of political thought in which much of the program and objectives, and even some of the strategy and tactics, have preceded the need—and the opportunity—to embody these in practice. The Neo-Guild Socialists who today are found in trade unions, in intellectual circles, and in a variety of political groupings, have reason to believe that a great deal of Cole's theory is capable of translation into action. Perhaps the major exception to such application is Cole's belief in a transitional period of state ownership of firms between the periods of private ownership and workers' control. Few supporters of workers' control are willing to trust the state with performance of this task, and are more willing to follow those instincts which are akin to Cole's well-stated misgivings on government.[26]

A further reason for Cole's preeminence, it must be admitted, is that the great body of his theoretical work has not been subjected to any test. Social and behavioral science have not achieved a level of methodological sophistication which could test his work with any assurance. The future may present an opportunity for the development of such a social laboratory, for certainly there are signs of movement toward workers' control, but it is most dubious that anything approaching a "pure" Cole model will ever evolve.[22] It is more appropriate to think of his contributions as important reference points.

The strength and resilience of the workers' control ideal also tend to underscore Cole's contributions to it, for quite apart from the efforts of Cole or of any other writer, it has long been looked upon as attractive and worthwhile. It had occurred to workers well before Cole came along, and it has enjoyed a continued, and even burgeoning, strength in the latter part of the twentieth century. The logic of workers proceeds along such lines as: "We do the work. We make the profits. We spend our lives here. We should be in control."[28] Carolyn Pateman, an Australian scholar who has devoted much of her research to the study of participation, believes that workers' control must be a vital part of any functioning democratic system. Democracy in the political system is not enough. Exclusion of the workplace from democratic decision-making processes is damaging to the functions of systems and is responsible for legitimating authoritarianism outside the work environment. Alienation derived from authoritarian workplace structures, in short, can lead to anti-social behavior and even to a societal breakdown.[29]

Pateman, in many ways, is echoing Cole in this part of her work, written more than fifty years after *Self-Government in Industry.* She has reiterated what might be an accurate observation, even a verity, of modern industrial society.

IV   *Decentralization and Local Control*

Cole's interest in workers' control forms only one part of a more broadly detailed political and social philosophy, for throughout his works, including those devoted to workers' control, there is an overriding concern and presumption in favor of small governing structures, one-to-one relationships between governor and governed, and decentralization.

He was not dogmatic in this attachment. He supported the necessity of large-scale organizations such as the United Nations, for example, and he recognized a need for government agencies to be large enough, both in terms of authority and in scope of jurisdiction, to perform such functions as transportation policymaking, pollution control, or the direction of foreign affairs. It was also taken for granted that certain types of industries require optimal scales of organization which go well beyond the ideal of small-scale, personal-level governance.

Wherever and whenever possible, though, Cole always insisted upon decision-making structures that are cohesive, responsible, accountable, and small. Parliament, it has been shown, did not meet these criteria, but it is also doubtful, for example, that the Greater London Council, a Tory invention that has come into its own since Cole's death, would measure up. Guild Socialism, as conceived by Cole, was to establish a responsible and accountable governance structure for the political system which would complement democratic control of industry.

A trend quite to the contrary was dominant during all of Cole's life, culminating in the heavy governmental direction characteristic of the New Deal and post–New Deal periods in the United States, the centralization and Keynesian planning of Western Europe, and the developments of Nazism and Stalinism. Decentralization, as well as democratic Socialism, appeared to be lost causes at the time of his death. Cole did not despair. Right up to his death, he continued his advocacy. He believed, as Rousseau did, that it is impossible for one person to represent another, that democracy required self-government, that all hierarchies must be disadvantaged with a presumption of their illegitimacy until some very good reason can be found to assert their necessity, and that in most cases no such reason exists.

A review of recent social–science literature, particularly in

Britain and the United States, shows a marked upsurge of interest in decentralization, community involvement, and neighborhood control of governmental services.[30] The newly organized rural and urban regional governments in Britain, the almost-universal interest in establishing ombudsman offices to provide a voice and appeals process for citizens outside regularized bureaucratic networks, the establishment of neighborhood city halls, the decentralization of services such as education and law enforcement, the emphasis upon sharing central government revenues with state and local governments, and actual experiments in neighborhood government all point to a new and countervailing trend. It is not the dominant trend, for the habit of centralization is ingrained and has a momentum of its own, often aided and abetted by politicians, bureaucrats, and special interests. Cole's steadfast support of local government and of the principles of community, or neighborhood, control have been an influence in maintaining their vitality over the many decades when the forces behind them were dormant.[31] It is not always possible to trace the impact of this contribution, but it is interesting to note that organizations such as the Portola Institute and People for Self-Management, which are involved in the revival of the workers' control movement, are also involved in community-control studies and efforts.

Community control and workers' control are such complementary concepts that this is scarcely surprising. In the case of Cole, they each provide an element of his regard for small political structures, face-to-face discussion and decisions, mistrust of remote centers of power, and a political fabric sewn together by a communal spirit. Community control and workers' control are brought together in many of the traditions revered by Cole—the Owenites, the cooperatives, the preindustrial guilds—and in the thought and contributions of social innovators like Owen, Ruskin, and Morris. The conflicts faced by each of these causes are also the same in essence, for the task of winning community control of political life is as great as that of winning workers' control of industrial life, and the forces aligned against them are both similar and overlapping. The importance of the two causes is also similar, and the experience gained in dealing with local issues and concerns can be applied, in a vital way, to the problems in larger frameworks:

Our problem . . . is to find democratic ways of living for little men in big societies. For men are little, and their capacity cannot transcend their experience, or grow except by continuous building upon their historic past. They can control great affairs only by acting together in the control of small affairs, and finding, through the experience of neighborhood, men whom they can entrust with larger decisions than they can take rationally for themselves. Democracy can work in the great State (and . . . between great States. . .) only if each State is made up of a host of little democracies, and rests finally, not on isolated individuals, but on groups small enough to express the spirit of neighbourhood and personal acquaintance.[32]

The question of local government, and of neighborhood control of local government, is therefore of transcendent significance to Cole, and though his philosophy of local government may suffer from a certain incompleteness, it can be seen that he produced an embryonic theory which served his overriding political philosophy well. Taken together with his substantial contributions and influence on the cause of workers' control, it tends to round out Cole as a full-fledged political philosopher whose writings provide a pertinent message for the overgoverned, centrally controlled citizens of twentieth-century industrial societies.

V   The Technological Question: Asking It

Cole's influence on the technological question, that most pervasive of twentieth-century issues, cannot be doubted, for he is one of the notable dissenters against the stated and unstated premises of technocratic advocates and planners. In addition, most of his important contributions on this question predate the rather more sophisticated treatments of thinkers such as Hannah Arendt, Herbert Marcuse, and Lewis Mumford. Much of Cole's work on this question has been reviewed elsewhere,[33] but it is prudent to delineate his two major points, which relate (1) to the materialism engendered by the so-called "progress" wrought by technology, and (2) to technology itself.

Though it may be considered strange for a Socialist, Cole does not believe in the primacy of materialism as the motive force behind initiatives for equality, for self-government, for industrial democracy, or for any of the social objectives he deems important. The relief of human want and misery through the provision of material needs is, of course, of great and even transcendent importance, for a society like William Morris envisioned, and which in turn inspired Cole, cannot be built upon hunger, poverty, or disease. Provision of material needs, however, cannot be an end in itself, in Cole's view, for he echoes the Scriptures by urging that humankind does not thrive on bread alone. There is a unity of purpose above and beyond this — in one place he calls it a spirit of fellowship — which defines human interaction and which sets the human species apart from others. It sounds almost religious, but it is not religious in any traditional sense, for Cole denies the concept of God and instead emphasizes that the highest and most singular devotion of humankind must be to one another. But materialism not only fails as the highest goal; it also fails as an explanation of history or of social and political action, not because it is not consequential but because no single factor can serve such an abstract purpose. This view is wrong in the eyes of many Socialists, but it links Cole with some of the New Left thinkers and with others, including some Neo-Marxists, whom he preceded. It also points up Cole's strong and successful attempt to be nondogmatic in his analysis.

The question of technology itself is no lesser quandary, but Cole's chief legacy in this sphere is his unwillingness to accept the premise that a technological innovation should be implemented simply because this is possible. A world faced with destruction from ecological deterioration or from nuclear disaster can well understand this position, but it is not the easy stance that it may seem; the onlookers laughed at Robert Fulton and his steamboat, but the rest of us have laughed at them ever since. To one born into a Victorian era suffused with the idea of "progress," with building, industrialization, and incredible optimism on every hand, with a world map largely pink with the imperialist expansionism of his country, and with even the time by which the world set its clocks decided just down the river at Greenwich, it was heretical to be so dubious. Cole knew however, what others would only realize later: that one did not have to be a Luddite to recognize that many of the processes of industrialization and technology violate the spirit of craftsmanship, that routinization of tasks creates dullness in the workplace and numbness in the mind, that workers want to see the result, the product, of their labor, and that ignoring these considerations leads to alienation and perhaps to societal disintegration.

Cole was not naive about technology. He recognized its obvious benefits. He only wished to see it develop in an orderly fashion in which the human equation would remain the uppermost consideration. The history of industrialization, as well as of subsidiary matters such as highway construction, weapons technology, and the deliberate manufacture of obsolescence, tends to underscore the legitimacy and relevance of his concern. His position has been one of unique and lasting influence, and, most importantly, it appears that it may now be appreciated and even applied.

VI *Appraisal*

The years since his death have seen G. D. H. Cole loom larger than ever as a literate and formidable social and political philosopher, and to some extent as a prophet. Cole's legacies are important enough to insure that he will never slide into the shadows of the forgotten, but they have acquired new dimensions, meanings, and timeliness which few people, perhaps not even Cole himself, could foresee.

Whether he was a prophet is conjectural. He is surely wrong about all sorts of things—how the British political and economic systems would change or the prospects for peace at one time or another. Some of the foreign-policy speculations he allowed himself to indulge in—Cole was a great one for writing "whither?" articles—appear positively ludicrous to some of those who have the benefit of crystalline hindsight.[34] This is of no consequence. Cole is not likely to be remembered for his foreign-policy speculations or for his predictions concerning contemporary events.

His major legacies are found in the persistent and consistent themes of his works, and the reasoned analyses and moral presumptions behind these themes—on society, on technology, on democracy, and on economics—bear some prophetic attributes. Put another way, it can be said that Cole's positions have achieved a new and well-warranted strength in the light of Western experience since his death. Viewpoints and solutions that are quite like Cole's, or which have been influenced by Cole, are heard on major issues of equality, bureaucracy, job satisfaction, size and responsiveness of governmental units, "progress," representation, and distrust of political power. The

Guild Socialist outlook he so skillfully enunciated takes on new meaning with the rise of the multi-national corporation, the increasing gap between rich and poor, the facelessness of large-scale organizations, the pervasiveness of military-industrial-governmental combines, and the increasing alienation associated with work routines. The emphasis which Cole placed upon craftsmanship has its counterpart in the significance of arts and crafts that is found in the "counterculture." [35] This value has also found renewed acceptance at a more general level in Western societies, taking such forms as the interest in antiques and various "nostalgia" relics, and in revived crafts and skills.

Some of the characteristics of large-scale institutions have changed in form, so that Cole's works and concerns must be observed through temporal prisms, but they have not changed *in esse*. Governments may be slightly less inclined to resort to overt repression or violence if their aims appear achievable by other means; there are public–relations costs to be considered in the media-conscious world. Workplace alienation is more likely to take a psychological form, and workers are more afflicted by a Kafkaesque sense of purposelessness than by a physical bone tiredness. The strain of manual labor has been partially superseded by the strain born of manipulative mechanisms. [36] Trade unions have continued to gain wider acceptance even as they become more bureaucratic and reactionary.

Cole's concern over such issues remains valid and even prophetic, because they have not substantively changed, and because he perceived their enormity, their centrality, and their repercussions upon the lives of individuals.

If the essentials of the problems Cole sought to address remain intact, giving his work a certain timelessness as well as timeliness, and if Cole was really insightful on these major problems and issues, an obvious question remains: why has he been largely unheeded? Why have few, if any, of Cole's major prescriptions for social change been adopted? [37] Britain, the United States, and most Western societies can be characterized as capitalist, imperialist (at least from an economic standpoint), centralist, based upon privilege and sometimes even upon caste, bureaucratic, and wasteful of both human and material resources. Workers' control remains at the periphery of most of these societies, and the technological question is being asked only after technology has been allowed to defile and ravage the physical environment upon which humankind must depend. Cole's battles and causes, in the main, have been on the losing side.

Cole's life and works encompass this major element of tragedy. Dame Margaret Cole has stated, with considerable assurance, that he was able to live with this. He may have expected to be on the losing side most of the time, for he knew the odds were unpromising in a society built upon a rigid class structure, an imperialist foreign policy, and a capitalist economic system. One way Cole managed to deal with his disappointment is found in his flexibility—his temperate and tolerant approach to life—for he was able to make some adjustments. He did not believe that he had any special pathway to truth, and his nondogmatic character has been amply illustrated. Some observers may even believe that there is a considerable difference between the "older" and "younger" Cole. There is no doubt that Cole did change some of his views over time, particularly on foreign policy, but the major contributions to political and social thought that he made over a period of five decades—from *Self-Government in Industry* to *A History of Socialist Thought*—are most remarkable for their steady reliance upon principles which assume, above all else, a character of constancy. Cole is paradoxically flexible and tolerant while also exhibiting a resolute constancy of purpose.

This does not answer the question of Cole's tragedy, but it helps to illuminate the wider tragedy. The cooperative commonwealth which Cole sought would not have given its citizens a utopian existence, not could it have been a guarantor of peace, prosperity, happiness, and all of those ingredients of life which humankind eternally desires; but it may have lessened the chances for the societal conflict and misery which have been a plague since the onset of recorded time. The sweep of twentieth-century history shows that it provided little hope or opportunity to bring such a society into being.

Notes and References

Chapter One

1. This idea was first suggested to the author by James Christoph, a political scientist at Indiana University, and it appears to possess a great deal of validity.

2. G. D. H. Cole, *William Morris as a Socialist* (London, 1960), p. 4.

3. S. T. Glass, *The Responsible Society: The Idea of Guild Socialism* (London, 1966), pp. 6-9.

4. Interview with Dame Margaret Cole, Ealing, June 1, 1973.

5. Fabius was a Roman warrior. In encountering Hannibal, he delayed taking action until the opportune time, though censured by his followers for the delay. But when he struck, he struck hard, so that his long wait was not in vain. Some ask when the Fabians have ever struck hard; others ask whether the blow is still pending; Alexander Gray, *The Socialist Tradition, Moses to Lenin* (London, 1946), p. 386.

6. Margaret Cole, *The Story of Fabian Socialism* (Stanford, 1961), pp. 7-9.

7. Margaret Cole has edited the diaries of Beatrice Webb and has devoted considerable writing to the Webbs as her subject; see Beatrice Webb, *Diaries 1912-24* and *Diaries 1924-32*, both edited by Margaret Cole (London, 1952), and *The Webbs And Their Work*, ed. Margaret Cole (Hassocks, 1974 revised edition).

8. See the comparison of the two in Margaret Cole, *The Story of Fabian Socialism*, pp. 252-58.

9. G. D. H. Cole, *James Keir Hardie* (London, 1941 pamphlet).

10. *Oxford Socialist*, November 14, 1942 (not paginated).

11. Margaret Cole, *The Life of G. D. H. Cole* (New York, 1971), p. 189; G. D. H. Cole and Raymond Postgate, *The British Common People, 1746-1946* (London, 1961), pp. 587-94.

12. Manuscript, Cole Collection, Nuffield College, Oxford, prepared for *Left News*, January 9, 1943; also undated manuscript, "Socialisation and Workers' Control," Cole Collection.

13. Interview with Dame Margaret Cole, Ealing, June 1, 1973.

14. Manuscript, "Labour's Immediate Ideal for Industry," undated, Cole Collection.

15. Margaret Cole, *Growing Up Into Revolution* (London, 1949), pp. 144-52.

16. G. D. H. Cole, *The British Cooperative Movement in a Socialist Society* (London, 1951), pp. 155-61. Cole's chief contribution in this field is *A Century of Cooperation* (London, 1944).

17. G. D. H. Cole, "Thoughts After the Election," *New Statesman and Nation*, 49 (1955), 875-76.

Chapter Two

1. (London, 1960), p. 1.

2. Kingsley Martin obituary, "G. D. H. Cole," *New Statesman*, 57 (1959), 63.

3. A. J. P. Taylor, "A Bolshevik Soul in a Fabian Muzzle," *New Statesman*, 82 (1971), 441-42.

4. He was occasionally called "O," especially at Balliol College, because of a strange way in which a professor called the roll; Ivor Brown, "G. D. H. Cole as an Undergraduate," in *Essays in Labour History: In Memory of G. D. H. Cole*, ed. Asa Briggs and John Saville (London, 1960), p. 3.

5. Margaret Cole, *The Life of G. D. H. Cole* (New York, 1971), chapters 1-4.

6. Ivor Brown, "G. D. H. Cole as an Undergraduate," p. 5.

7. *Ibid.*, pp. 3-5; A. J. P. Taylor, "A Bolshevik Soul in a Fabian Muzzle."

8. *The Story of Fabian Socialism* (Stanford, 1961); *Growing Up into Revolution* (London, 1949); Beatrice Webb, *Diaries 1912-24* and *Diaries 1924-32*, both edited by Margaret Cole (London, 1952); Margaret Cole, *The Life of G. D. H. Cole*.

9. *Life of GDHC*, p. 90.

10. *Life of GDHC*, Chapters 8, 13, and 14.

11. G. D. H. Cole, *The Meaning of Marxism* (London, 1948), p. 290.

12. Manuscript, undated and untitled, Cole Collection, Nuffield College, Oxford.

13. Letter from Sunshine, Victoria, Australia, dated May 30, 1972.

14. Stephen K. Bailey, "What Cole Really Meant," in *Essays in Labour History*, p. 23.

15. *Ibid.*

16. Jean-Jacques Rosseau, *The Social Contract and Discourses* (New York, 1932). This continues to go through one printing after another.

17. All of these works are cited in the bibliography.

18. Hugh Gaitskell, "At Oxford in the Twenties," in *Essays in Labour History*, pp. 18-19.

19. On the pervasiveness of politics in our lives see Alan Wolfe and Charles A. McCoy, *Political Analysis: An Unorthodox Approach* (New York, 1972), Preface and p. xiii.

20. Anne Fremantle, *This Little Band of Prophets: The British Fabians* (New York, 1960), pp. 209-10. According to the Fremantle

account, Beatrice Webb predicted during this meeting that Cole would someday become Prime Minister.

21. Paul Thompson, *Socialists, Liberals and Labour: The Struggle for London, 1885-1914* (London, 1967), p. 219.

22. S. T. Glass, *The Responsible Society: The Ideas of Guild Socialism* (London, 1966), pp. 25-37.

23. *Ibid.*, Chapter 2 and pp. 41-42.

24. Georges Sorel, *Reflections on Violence* (New York, 1950), especially the Introduction and Chapter 5.

25. Margaret Cole, *Story of Fabian Socialism*, p. 220.

26. Anne Fremantle, *Little Band of Prophets*, p. 170.

27. S. T. Glass, *The Responsible Society*, pp. 17-21.

28. This is strongly in evidence in the debates and proceedings of the National Guilds League; for example, *Verbatim Proceedings, National Guilds League 1917 Annual Conference*, Cole Collection.

29. *Verbatim Proceedings, National Guilds League 1920 Annual Conference*, p. 1, Cole Collection.

30. S. T. Glass, *The Responsible Society*, p. 39 and Chapters 5 and 6.

31. Letter from G. D. H. Cole to Beatrice Webb dated September 26, 1939. A separate list, which like this letter is in the Cole Collection, had a Glasgow Clerks Guild, an Aberdeen Dockers Guild, a Horticultural Nursery Guild in Waltham Cross, Hertfordshire, and Guilds of Engineering (machine-shop workers) in London and Coventry.

32. Margaret Cole, *Life of G. D. H. Cole*, pp. 158-60.

33. Volume IV, Part 1 (London, 1958), 443-55.

34. *Life of GDHC*, p. 183.

36. Manuscript, untitled and undated (c. 1936), Cole Collection.

37. Most of these are economic speculation and are mistakes of degree rather than kind; he assuredly had good sense in economics on the matter of fighting the Depression. His worst overall mistake was in opposing rearmament against Germany, but this emanated from his pacifistic and Little Englander roots.

38. G. D. H. Cole and Margaret Cole, *A Guide to Modern Politics* (New York, 1934), pp. 190-94.

39. G. D. H. Cole, "Why We Should Not Reduce Wages," *New Statesman and Nation*, 1 (1931), 453-54, 483-84; G. D. H. Cole, "Mr. Keynes Beats the Band" (review of *The General Theory of Employment, Interest and Money*), *New Statesman and Nation*, 11 (1936), 220-22. But "To his [Cole's] way of thinking the enthusiasm for Keynes . . . was quite excessive: all Keynes was doing was to re-state what Hobson had said some thirty years before. In any case the whole business was only tinkering: the structure of capitalism had developed cracks far deeper and wider than could be papered over with mere changes in monetary and budgetary practice." G. D. N. Worswick, "Cole and Oxford, 1938-1958," in *Essays in Labour History*, p. 27.

40. G. D. H. Cole and Margaret Cole, *A Guide to Modern Politics,* pp. 127-46.

41. *The Meaning of Marxism* (London, 1948); also available in an Ann Arbor Paperback Edition (Ann Arbor, 1964). The first edition was published by Gollancz in 1934 under the title of *What Marx Really Meant.* See Chapter 4.

42. Margaret Cole, *Life of G. D. H. Cole,* p. 229.

43. *Life of GDHC,* Chapters 18 and 19; Margaret Cole, *Story of Fabian Socialism,* pp. 218-42.

44. Cole complains about this in an undated manuscript, "Flying Fame," found in the Cole Collection.

45. Margaret Cole, *Life of GDHC,* p. 233.

46. Morris and Austin cars are manufactured by British Motors works at Cowley, near Oxford, and this William Morris is not to be confused with the great nineteenth-century Socialist writer.

47. Margaret Cole, *Life of GDHC,* pp. 235-52; G. D. H. Cole, "The Nuffield College Social Reconstruction Survey: A Description," *Social Welfare* (of Manchester and Salford) 5 (1942), 37-42; G. D. N. Worswick, "Cole and Oxford, 1938-1958," in *Essays in Labour History,* pp. 30-36.

48. Margaret Cole, *Life of GDHC,* p. 18 and Chapters 21-24.

49. This university representation might be said to be the only "functional representation" still existing in the House of Commons at this time. The abolition of university seats, which were obviously a holdover from an unreformed Parliament and were simply another elite mechanism, should be considered the last minor reform in the great chain which was established in 1832 and had been mostly accomplished by the reforms of 1911 and 1928. The Labour government of 1945-1951 did away with this anachronism.

50. G. D. H. Cole, "Debate on Steel—The Case for Nationalisation," *The Banker,* 88 (1948), 149-60.

51. Margaret Cole, *Story of Fabian Socialism,* p. 316.

52. Interview with Dame Margaret Cole, Ealing, June 1, 1973.

53. Gabriel and Joyce Kolko, *The Limits of Power: The World and United States Foreign Policy, 1945-1954* (New York, 1972).

54. G. D. H. Cole, "Socialists and Communism," *New Statesman and Nation,* 51 (1956), 472-74.

55. G. D. H. Cole, "As a Socialist Sees It," *New Statesman and Nation,* 41 (1951), 120-21; G. D. H. Cole, "As a Socialist Sees It" (a letter), *New Statesman and Nation,* 41 (1951), 216-17.

56. Manuscript, untitled and undated (c. 1936), Cole Collection.

57. This of course is only a general impression, but it appears to be true.

58. G. D. H. Cole, "My Books," *Swinton and Pendlebury Public Libraries Bulletin,* 8 (January 1935), pp. 4-5.

59. *Ibid.*

60. *Ibid.*

61. *Ibid.*

62. Interview with Dame Margaret Cole, Ealing, June 1, 1973.

63. Galley proof, untitled and undated (c. 1946), Cole Collection.

64. Interview with Dame Margaret Cole, Ealing, June 1, 1973.

65. See Michael Foot's two-volume *Aneurin Bevan: A Biography* (London, 1962). Aneurin Bevan also has an autobiography, *In Place of Fear* (London, 1952).

66. Dame Margaret Cole, interview, Ealing, June 1, 1973. This does not mean that he was critical of Bevan; for example, see G. D. H. Cole, "The Labour Party and the Trade Unions," *Political Quarterly*, 24 (1953), 22–23.

67. Interview with Dame Margaret Cole, Ealing, June 1, 1973; Margaret Cole, *The Life of GDHC*; Hugh Gaitskell, "At Oxford in the Twenties," in *Essays in Labour History*, pp. 6–19.

68. Interview with Dame Margaret Cole, Ealing, June 1, 1973.

69. Letter from Dame Margaret Cole, dated July 29, 1966.

70. Hugh Gaitskell, "At Oxford in the Twenties," in *Essays in Labour History*, p. 9.

71. A. J. P. Taylor, "A Bolshevik Soul in a Fabian Muzzle." This poem also appears in *Life of GDHC*, p. 207.

72. A. J. P. Taylor, "A Bolshevik Soul," and Kingsley Martin, "G. D. H. Cole," p. 63.

Chapter Three

1. "National management" would not be necessary in all circumstances, however; it would be important in those industries and activities of crucial importance to the economy whose workers were advanced in militancy, such as railways and mining; see Cole's *Self-Government in Industry* (1917; reissued in London, 1972) and *Guild Socialism Restated* (London, 1920); also S. T. Glass, *The Responsible Society: The Ideas of Guild Socialism* (London, 1966), pp. 41–45. It is interesting to note how much beyond the pale this idea is now viewed in literature and discussions on workers' control. A proposed intermediate period of state control between the stages of private ownership and workers' control was given short shrift by all of the speakers and participants in a panel on workers' control at the September 1974 Annual Meeting of the American Political Science Association in Chicago.

2. The foregoing is primarily based upon *Self-Government in Industry* and *Guild Socialism Restated*, Cole's two most important theoretical works on Guild Socialism.

3. Hannah Arendt, *The Human Condition* (Chicago, 1958); Jacques Ellul, *The Technological Society* (New York, 1964); Paul Goodman,

Growing Up Absurd (New York, 1960); Herbert Marcuse, *One-Dimensional Man* (Boston, 1964) and *An Essay on Liberation* (Boston, 1969); Lewis Mumford, *The City in History: Its Origins, Its Transformation and Its Prospects* (New York, 1961); Theodore Roszak, *The Making of a Counter-Culture* (Garden City, 1969); Kirkpatrick Sale, *SDS: Ten Years Toward a Revolution* (New York, 1973); Alvin Toffler, *Future Shock* (New York, 1970).

4. G. D. H. Cole, *William Morris as a Socialist* (London, 1960), p. 10.

5. G. D. H. Cole, *Self-Government in Industry*, pp. 83–124; S. G. Hobson and A. R. Orage, "The Bondage of Wagery" and "State and Municipal Wagery," in *Industrial Democracy in Great Britain: A Book of Readings and Witnesses for Workers' Control*, eds. Ken Coates and Tony Topham (London, 1968), pp. 40–45.

6. *Industrial Democracy in Great Britain; Can the Workers Run Industry?*, ed. Ken Coates (London, 1968); David Jenkins, *Job Power: Blue and White Collar Democracy* (Garden City, 1973); *Industrial Democracy and Canadian Labour*, eds. Leo Roback *et al.* (Toronto, 1968); for an international review, see Adolf F. Sturmthal, *Workers Councils* (Cambridge, 1966).

7. Studs Terkel, *Working: People Talk About What They Do All Day and How They Feel About What They Do* (New York, 1974); Kenneth Lasson, *The Workers* (New York, 1973).

8. G. D. H. Cole, untitled and undated manuscript, Cole Collection, Nuffield College, Oxford.

9. G. D. H. Cole, *Self-Government in Industry*, Chapters 1 and 2.

10. Some of the foregoing summary is suggested by S. T. Glass, *The Responsible Society*, pp. 4–9, 17–24.

11. *Ibid.*, p. 39; Margaret Cole, *The Life of G. D. H. Cole* (New York, 1971), pp. 74–75. A. R. Orage, the editor of the Guild paper *New Age*, was a man of notable talents who made a lasting contribution to the Guild movement through his stewardship of this publication during the years from 1907 to 1922. He has been hailed as a great editor of the twentieth century who produced a paper as acclaimed for its literary quality as for its political content. In addition to writers one might expect to see because of Fabian or Guild Socialist connections—Cole, Webb, Shaw, Wells, and Hobson—it included contributions of Hilare Belloc, Arnold Bennett, Ambrose Bierce, G. K. Chesterton, Havelock Ellis, John Galsworthy, Frank Harris, Katherine Mansfield, Ezra Pound, and Siegfried Sassoon. Artwork by Picasso and by Wyndham Lewis graced its pages. Orage, though he later turned to Douglas Credit, was for a time a convinced Guild Socialist who, though he was very well acquainted with Marxism and with the values of Benthamism and science which had been so prevalent in Victorian England, was an enthusiastic believer in aesthetic Socialism as represented by William

Morris. Characterized as one whose "need to follow was as great as his need to lead," he was invariably associated with unsuccessful causes. He was greatly mourned by Cole upon his death in 1934; see Chapter 4, "Orage and the *New Age,*" in Samuel Hynes,*Edwardian Occasions: Essays on English Writing in the Early Twentieth Century* (New York, 1972).

12. Arthur Gleason, quoted by editor John Corina in the 1972 edition of *Self-Government in Industry,* pp. 257–58.

13. See the discussion of *Self-Government in Industry* in Chapter 4.

14. A basic conundrum of all pluralist theory is described by Ellen D. Ellis in "Guild Socialism and Pluralism," *American Political Science Review* 17 (1923), 585: "The pluralist, fixing his attention on the various forms of group life, which have existed within the body politic in the past, and which are developing with such bewildering complexity in the society of the present, sets out by denying that there exists or ever did exist the unitary sovereign state. Yet this denial having been made, there very generally appears a strange inconsistency, . . . for in spite of their protestations to the contrary, all the pluralists, except the syndicalists have . . . acknowledged that a unified absolute sovereignty as the ultimate controlling authority, has in fact been characteristic of the political organization of mankind, although they believe such authority to have been without justification. A further analysis of the writings of the pluralists, moreover, almost invariably reveals the curious and difficult confusion of state with government and of fact with right. . . ."

Cole's ability to handle this conundrum was clear enough in all of his writings on the state. A good example: "Of course, if by 'State' is meant merely any ultimate body, there is no more to be said: in this sense everyone who is not an Anarchist is an advocate of State Sovereignty. But if the sovereignty of the State means the sovereignty of Parliament with its subordinate local bodies, then I maintain that it is utterly inconsistent with the principle on which Guild Socialism rests." G. D. H. Cole, *Self-Government in Industry,* p. 14.

The development of pluralist theory over the past three decades has seen a closer tie to the state, to systems analysis models of the state and to systems maintenance bias. Examples of this literature include: Nelson W. Polsby, *Community Power and Political Theory* (New Haven, 1963); Robert A. Dahl, *A Preface to Democratic Theory* (Chicago, 1956); Robert A. Dahl, *Polyarchy: Participation and Opposition* (New Haven, 1971). A tie-in between this literature and concerns of Cole and the Guild Socialists can be seen in Robert A. Dahl, "Power to the Workers?"*New York Review of Books* 15 (November 19, 1970), pp. 20–24.

15. Nelson W. Polsby, *Community Power and Political Theory;* Seymour M. Lipset, *Political Man* (Garden City: 1963).

16. These themes pervade nearly all of Cole's writings; for a list of references, see the bibliography.

17. A few examples of his nonsectarian works include the *History of Socialist Thought*, 5 volumes (London, 1960) and *The Simple Case for Socialism* (London, 1935).

18. See John Corina's Introduction to the 1972 reissue of *Self-Government in Industry* and S. T. Glass, *The Responsible Society*.

19. G. D. H. Cole, *Persons and Periods: Studies* (London, 1938), pp. 143-95; G. D. H. Cole, *Chartist Portraits*, second ed., (London, 1965); G. D. H. Cole, *The Life of William Cobbett* (London, 1924).

20. *Ibid.;* also G. D. H. Cole, *Persons and Periods*, pp. 143-95.

21. *Ibid.*, pp. 196-215; G. D. H. Cole, *A Short History of the British Working Class Movement, 1789-1947* (London, 1947), pp. 75-81; G. D. H. Cole, *A Century of Cooperation* (Manchester, 1944), especially pp. 1-113.

22. G. D. H. Cole, *Robert Owen* (London, 1925).

23. G. D. H. Cole, *A Century of Cooperation*, pp. 1-113.

24. Clinton Rossiter, *Marxism: The View from America* (New York, 1960), p. 9.

25. Interview with Dame Margaret Cole, Ealing, June 1, 1973.

26. G. D. H. Cole and Margaret Cole, *A Guide to Modern Politics* (New York, 1934), pp. 177-94; G. D. H. Cole, *The Meaning of Marxism* (London, 1948); Cole's writings are replete with denunciations of Soviet police-state tactics and centralization.

27. G. D. H. Cole and Raymond Postgate, *The British Common People 1746-1946* (London, 1961), pp. 585-87.

28. Margaret Cole, *The Life of G. D. H. Cole*, p. 162.

29. G. D. H. Cole, "Wakeful Partners in Industry," *New Statesman*, 54 (1957), 373.

30. G. D. H. Cole, *The Principles of Socialism: A Syllabus for Study Circles*, second ed. (London, 1917, pamphlet), pp. 5-6.

31. Margaret Cole, *The Life of G. D. H. Cole*, p. 122.

32. Manuscript, undated and untitled, Cole Collection.

33. G. D. H. Cole, *William Morris as a Socialist*, p. 5.

34. G. D. H. Cole, "Guild Socialism and Communism," manuscript dated May 1921, Cole Collection, Nuffield College, Oxford.

35. *Ibid.;* this is a general theme in Cole's works.

36. *Ibid.*

37. G. D. H. Cole, *A Plan for Democratic Britain* (London, 1939), pp. 242-44.

38. On Laski, see Margaret Cole, *The Life of G. D. H. Cole*, p. 202; Max Beloff, "G. D. H. Cole—'Secular Saint'?" *Encounter* 38 (February, 1972), pp. 62-67.

39. Nigel Birch, *The Conservative Party* (London, 1949), p. 48.

40. G. D. H. Cole, *Self-Government in Industry*, especially Chapter

1; G. D. H. Cole, *Economic Tracts for the Times* (London, 1932), pp. 321-27. This is Cole's most important and most oft-repeated central thesis. It is found at some point in every work in which he deals with central theoretical questions of politics, economics, society, and culture.

41. Ludwig Von Mises, *Socialism* (New Haven, 1951), p. 258.

42. *Ibid.*, pp. 258-62.

43. G. D. H. Cole, *Self-Government in Industry*, Chapter 4.

44. From a series of four lectures prepared for delivery at Mortimer Hall in early 1921; Cole Collection. See especially pp. 4-5 of the second lecture.

45. "F. F.," "Guild Socialism—A Good Thing for Capitalist Ratepayers," *Socialist Standard*, 19 (1922), 194-95. An "A.E.R." (probably one A. E. Randall) believes that Cole is wrong in asserting incompatibility of the state with the Guild Socialist system in a short untitled article, *New Age* (1915), 590; the same "A. E. R." takes Cole to task on the question of a Guilds constitution, stating that his "equipoise" and "counterprise" ingredients will not work in practice because they do not take sufficient account of human nature, *New Age* (1915), 495. William Morris had an answer for this: "What human nature? The human nature of paupers, of slaves, of slave-holders or the human nature of wealthy free men? Which? Come tell me that?" He is quoted by John Corina in the Introduction to *Self-Government in Industry*, p. xxxii. Cole was also criticized by T. W. Pateman in a letter to the *New Age* (April 29, 1915), (page number removed), for viewing the function of Parliament as a "consumers' representative body. . . . Parliament has other functions than [this,] notably, of course, the administration of justice and . . . [providing] . . . for defense. . . . Thus Parliament has the function of balancing and coordinating the various interests in the community. Mr. Cole would claim that such a final authority cannot rest on a territorial basis, but it seems to me that such a basis is the soundest. . . . I cannot accept Mr. Cole's view that 'the sovereignty of the territorial association means the sovereignty of the consumer.' "

46. G. D. H. Cole, *The British Labour Movement—Retrospect and Prospect* (London, 1951, pamphlet).

47. *Ibid.*, pp. 10-11; G. D. H. Cole, *A Plan for Democratic Britain*, pp. 242-44; G. D. H. Cole, *A Guide to the Elements of Socialism* (London, 1947, pamphlet).

48. *Ibid.;* G. D. H. Cole, *Labour's Second Term* (London, 1949, pamphlet); G. D. H. Cole, *A Plan for Democratic Britain*.

49. G. D. H. Cole, "Thoughts After the Election," *New Statesman and Nation*, 49 (1955), 875-76; G. D. H. Cole, *The Simple Case for Socialism*, pp. 192-93, 250-51, 288.

50. G. D. H. Cole, *Economic Tracts for the Times* (London, 1932), p. 325.

51. *Ibid.*, p. 327.

52. G. D. H. Cole, *A Plan for Democratic Britain*, p. 35.

53. *Ibid.*, pp. 27–35.

54. *Ibid.*

55. Interview with Dame Margaret Cole, Ealing, June 1, 1973; see also G. D. H. Cole, "Labour's Opportunity," *New Statesman and Nation*, 5 (1933), 437–38.

56. Interview with Dame Margaret Cole, Ealing, June 1, 1973.

57. G. D. H. Cole, "Thoughts After the Election."

58. *Ibid.*

59. *Ibid.*

60. G. D. H. Cole, *The Intelligent Man's Guide to the Post-War World* (London, 1947), pp. 499–512. This not only applies to Britain, Cole pointed out.

Chapter Four

1. G. D. H. Cole, *Self-Government in Industry* (1917; reissued in London, 1972); G. D. H. Cole, *Guild Socialism Re-Stated* (London, 1920); G. D. H. Cole, *The Simple Case for Socialism* (London, 1935); G. D. H. Cole, *The Meaning of Marxism* (London, 1948); G. D. H. Cole, *History of Socialist Thought*, 5 volumes (London, 1960).

2. G. D. H. Cole, *The World of Labour* (1913; reprinted New York, 1973).

3. G. D. H. Cole, *Self-Government in Industry*, p. xiii.

4. *SGII*, p. 256.

5. *SGII*, pp. xi–xii.

6. *SGII*, pp. 187–99.

7. *SGII*, pp. 44–45, 67, 126, 161.

8. *SGII*, p. 185.

9. *SGII*, p. 161.

10. *SGII*, pp. 125–26, 150. On the inadequacy of Collectivism even as a consumer doctrine, see p. 7.

11. *SGII*, Chapter 1.

12. *SGII*, p. 6.

13. *SGII*, pp. 15–16.

14. *SGII*, pp. 15–16.

15. *SGII*, pp. 16–17.

16. *SGII*, p. 147.

17. *SGII*, pp. 125–26.

18. G. D. H. Cole, "The Essentials of Socialisation," *Political Quarterly*, 2 (1931), 394–410.

19. *SGII*, pp. 125–26. Labour party campaigning for the 1974 elections indicated a strong and continuous attachment to Collectivism.

20. *SGII*, pp. 32–33.

21. *SGII*, p. 33.

22. *SGII*, p. xxix; on the historic debate within the Labour party between Collectivists and advocates of workers' control, see Robert A. Dahl, "Workers' Control of Industry and the British Labour Party," *American Political Science Review*, 41 (1947), 875–900.

23. *Self-Government in Industry*, pp. 45–47; Adolf F. Sturmthal, *Unity and Diversity in European Labor* (Glencoe, 1953); Andre Gorz, *Strategy for Labor: A Radical Proposal* (Boston, 1967).

24. For an example of this prescriptive approach, see *Self-Government in Industry*, p. 57.

25. *SGII*, pp. 63–64, xiv.

26. *SGII*, p. 65.

27. *SGII*, Chapter 3.

28. *SGII*, pp. 103–104.

29. G. D. H. Cole, "Retreat from Bigness," *New Statesman and Nation*, 55 (1958), 366–67.

30. *Self-Government in Industry*, pp. 84–85.

31. *SGII*, Chapter 4.

32. *SGII*, p. 157.

33. *SGII*, p. 157.

34. *SGII*, pp. xxv, xxxi.

35. See also Herbert Marcuse, *One-Dimensional Man* (Boston, 1964).

36. *Self-Government in Industry*, p. xxxi.

37. *SGII*, p. xxxii.

38. *SGII*, pp. 159–60.

39. G. D. H. Cole, *Guild Socialism Re-Stated* (London, 1920), p. 65.

40. *GSR*, p. 65.

41. *GSR*, pp. 65–66.

42. *GSR*, p. 24.

43. *GSR*, p. 29.

44. *GSR*, p. 30.

45. *GSR*, pp. 38–39.

46. *GSR*, p. 39.

47. *GSR*, p. 57.

48. *GSR*, p. 25.

49. See Part I of this Chapter.

50. *GSR*, pp. 120–25.

51. *GSR*, pp. 128–29.

52. *GSR*, pp. 128–29.

53. *GSR*, p. 216.

54. *GSR*, p. 75.

55. *GSR*, pp. 75–76.

56. *GSR*, p. 76.

57. *GSR*, p. 76.

58. *The Simple Case for Socialism*, p. 7.

59. *SCFS*, p. 8.
60. *SCFS*, p. 14.
61. *SCFS*, pp. 12–13.
62. *SCFS*, pp. 176–77.
63. *SCFS*, Chapter 2, especially pp. 19–20.
64. *SCFS*, p. 22.
65. *SCFS*, Chapter 3.
66. *SCFS*, p. 122.
67. *SCFS*, p. 122.
68. *Self-Government in Industry*, p. 142.
69. *The Simple Case for Socialism*, p. 197.
70. *SCFS*, pp. 197–99.
71. *SCFS*, p. 201.
72. *SCFS*, p. 174.
73. *SCFS*, p. 200.
74. *SCFS*, p. 202.
75. *SCFS*, p. 163.
76. *SCFS*, pp. 83–84.
77. *SCFS*, p. 160.
78. *SCFS*, p. 160.
79. *SCFS*, pp. 163–71.
80. Herbert Morrison, *Government and Parliament*, 3rd ed. (New York, 1964).
81. *The Simple Case for Socialism*, p. 155
82. *SCFS*, p. 252.
83. *SCFS*, pp. 256–57.
84. *SCFS*, p. 257.
85. *SCFS*, p. 259.
86. *SCFS*, p. 263.
87. *SCFS*, pp. 263–64.
88. *SCFS*, pp. 263–64.
89. G.D.H. Cole, *The Meaning of Marxism* (London, 1948); Lewis S. Feuer, *Marx and the Intellectuals: A Set of Post-Ideological Essays* (Garden City, 1969), p. 301, makes the assertion that Cole turned Marx into an English Realist.
90. G. D. H. Cole, *What Marx Really Meant* (London, 1934).
91. G. D. H. Cole, *A History of Socialist Thought*, I (London, 1961).
92. *The Meaning of Marxism*, p. 11.
93. *MOM*, p. 12.
94. *MOM*, p. 13.
95. *MOM*, pp. 12–13.
96. *MOM*, pp. 14–15.
97. For example, see *Saul Alinsky, Rules for Radicals* (New York, 1971).
98. *The Meaning of Marxism*, pp. 17–32, 77, and Chapter 2.

99. *MOM*, p. 33.
100. *MOM*, pp. 17–23, 27–32, and Chapter 2.
101. *Basic Writings on Politics and Philosophy: Karl Marx and Friedrich Engels*, ed. Lewis S. Feuer (Garden City, 1959), p. 6.
102. *Ibid.*, p. 41; Cole's specific criticisms of the *Manifesto* on this count are in *The Meaning of Marxism*, pp. 44–45. See also Chapter 12, "The Communist Manifesto of 1848," in G. D. H. Cole, *Essays in Social Theory* (London, 1950).
103. *The Meaning of Marxism*, p. 151.
104. *MOM*, pp. 92–93.
105. *MOM*, pp. 24, 40.
106. *MOM*, p. 48.
107. *MOM*, pp. 49–50.
108. *MOM*, pp. 269–90.
109. *MOM*, pp. 196–97.
110. *MOM*, pp. 198–99.
111. John H. Goldthorpe *et al.*, *The Affluent Worker in the Class Structure* (Cambridge, 1969).
112. *History of Socialist Thought*, V, p. ix.
113. V, p. ix.
114. V, p. ix, and Preface of Volume IV.
115. Hugh Gaitskell, "At Oxford in the Twenties," in *Essays in Labour History: In Memory of G. D. H. Cole*, eds. Asa Briggs and John Saville (London, 1960), p. 8.
116. Volume IV, pp. 10, 26. Of interest in connection with this section is a listing provided by Cole of other movements which he felt were exemplary of Guild Socialist tendencies: the early Histadrut movement of Israel, the "Plumb Plan" for American railways, the Catalonian version of Anarcho-Syndicalism which was so prominent in connection with the Spanish Civil War, the French movement for industrial nationalization, and small movements for workers' control in many countries of the world, including Russia.
117. Volume I, p. vi.
118. I, pp. 247–62.
119. Volume III, pp. 498–518.
120. III, p. 382.
121. See Chapter Five.
122. Volume III, p. 386.
123. III, pp. 286–87.
124. Volume IV, pp. 2–3.
125. IV, pp. 16–17, 22–23.
126. IV, p. 14, and Volume V, pp. 257–58.
127. Volume V, p. 258. Trotsky was later murdered by Stalin's henchmen while he was in exile.
128. V, p. 212.

129. Volume IV, pp. 10-12. Cole supported the views of the Centre Group, but he did not share their faith in these views.

130. See pp. 317-19.

131. Volume IV, pp. 384-90.

132. Paul Sweezy, "Professor Cole's *History of Socialist Thought,*" *American Economic Review,* 47 (1957), 986, 990-91.

133. Volume V, p. xi.

134. G. D. H. Cole, *Workshop Organisation,* ed. A. Marsh (London, 1973 edition).

135. G. D. H. Cole, *A Century of Cooperation* (London, 1944).

136. G. D. H. Cole, *Studies in Class Structure* (London, 1955); W. L. Guttsman, *The British Political Elite* (London, 1963).

137. G. D. H. Cole, *The World of Labour* (1913); (rpt. New York, 1973).

138. G. D. H. Cole, *The People's Front* (London, 1937).

139. G. D. H. Cole, *Economic Tracts for the Times* (London, 1932).

140. G. D. H. Cole, *Socialist Economics* (London, 1950).

141. G. D. H. Cole, *Essays in Social Theory* (London, 1950).

142. G. D. H. Cole, "Thoughts After the Election," *New Statesman and Nation,* 49 (1955), 875-76.

Chapter Five

1. This rather obvious point is made by Kingsley Martin in his obituary, "G. D. H. Cole," *New Statesman and Nation,* 57 (1959), 63.

2. See Chapter 4.

3. See Chapter 3.

4. The term "utopian" is used in a broad sense in this particular context.

5. Volume 5, *Socialism and Fascism, 1931-1939* (London, 1961), p. 337.

6. It is true that trade unions hold a predominant position, in terms of numbers, in the Annual Conference of the British Labour party, but the Conference—although it is considered the party's supreme authority—has generally held a position of less importance than the party's Parliamentary Caucus. The MPs and Leadership are not only given wide latitude by the extra-Parliamentary organization of the party; they also have held sway on some important policy questions when they were in fact thwarting the party's "official" policy. See Ralph Miliband, *Parliamentary Socialism* (London, 1961); Robert McKenzie, *British Political Parties* (London, 1963); Leon Epstein, "Who Makes Party Policy: British Labour, 1960-61," *Midwest Journal of Political Science,* 6 (1962), 165-82.

7. John Corina, "Introduction," in G. D. H. Cole, *Self-Government in Industry* (London, 1972 edition), p. xxix.

8. See Chapter 3.

9. Alan Whitehorn, "Alienation and Workers' Self-Management," *Canadian Slavonic Papers* (1974), 160–86; see especially p. 164.

10. This is a persistent theme in Yugoslav government materials which depict the country's economic system; for example, see *Yugoslav Facts and Views,* 92 (July 1974), p. 2; for a good introduction to this system that is sound, scholarly, and inclusive of interesting comparisons, see G. David Garson, *On Democratic Administration and Socialist Self-Management: A Comparative Survey Emphasizing the Yugoslav Experience* (Beverly Hills, 1974).

11. Kingsley Martin, "G. D. H. Cole," p. 63.

12. David Jenkins, *Job Power: Blue and White Collar Democracy* (Baltimore, 1974), Chapter 7.

13. Alan Whitehorn, "Workers' Self-Management: Socialist Myth or Prognostication?," unpublished paper delivered at the Annual Meeting, of the Meeting of the American Political Science Association, Chicago, September 1974 (available on microfilm).

14. Stephen Sachs, "Self Management as the Core of an Effective Program to Eliminate Poverty in the United States," unpublished paper delivered at the National Conference on Workers Self-Management, Boston, January 1974.

15. An earlier attempt is Adolf F. Sturmthal, *Workers Councils* (Cambridge, 1966).

16. See *Participatory Democracy for Canada,* ed. Jerry Hunnius (Montreal, 1971), especially the essay by André Gorz.

17. In recent years the movement has developed a strong focus of opposition to union bureaucracies through publication of periodicals such as *Voice of the Unions* and *Engineering Voice.* The latter contains the motto "Workers' Control" in its masthead. The officers of Britain's two largest unions, the TGWU and the AUEW, have been influenced to the point of endorsing the principle of workers' control, and a 1974 British Government White Paper has endorsed the principle of workers' representation on the boards of directors of limited liability (corporate) firms; Walter Kendall, "Workers Control: Useful TUC Plan Can Be Bigger," *Engineering Voice* (August 1974), p. 6; also Walter Kendall, *Workers' Participation and Workers' Control: Aspects of British Experience* (Oxford, 1974).

18. Most European countries make provisions for worker representation on company boards or in national contractual negotiations, however; a good short summary of these arrangements is Innis Macbeath, *The European Approach to Worker-Management Relationships* (Washington, D.C. 1973). The difficulty with most of these arrangements, from a Cole or Guild Socialist point of view, is that they involve no particular workshop democracy, and highly centralized bodies, quite remote from worker and workplace, do the important decision-making.

19. A preliminary report on the Triumph motorcycle works appears in *People for Self Management Newsletter,* 8-9 (July-October 1974), p. 5; the Clydeside shipbuilders' story is set out by Willie Thompson and Finlay Hart, *The UCS Work-In* (London, 1972).

20. Walter Kendall, *Workers' Participation and Workers' Control,* p. 70.

21. "It cannot be nothing to men how they spend all their working days. It is not really possible to treat the relations between men in their working day as though they did not affect their social relations." A. D. Lindsay, *The Modern Democratic State* (New York, 1962), p. 186.

22. David Jenkins, *Job Power,* Chapter 10.

23. Innis Macbeath, "The European Approach to Worker-Management Relationships," pp. 79-86.

24. John Corina, "Introduction," in *Self-Government in Industry;* Alan Whitehorn, "The Prospects for Workers' Self-Management in North America: Guild Socialism Revisited," unpublished paper delivered at the National Conference on Workers Self-Management, Boston, January 1974.

25. At least until one remembers the 1917 publication date of *Self-Government in Industry.*

26. For example, see G. D. H. Cole, "Retreat from Bigness," *New Statesman and Nation,* 55 (1958), 366-67.

27. The problem of identifying any model as a "Cole model" would be a very great one, since his thoughts on workers' control, though consistent on major themes throughout his life, were not always the same in every detail.

28. *Engineering Voice* (August 1974), p. 6.

29. As quoted by David Jenkins, *Job Power,* pp. 60-61. Pateman, whose work has centered upon participatory democracy, feels that the term "workers' control" is rather meaningless.

30. Milton Kotler, *Neighborhood Control: The Local Foundations of Political Life* (Indianapolis, 1969); Alan Altshuler, *Community Control: The Black Demand for Participation in Large American Cities* (New York, 1969); André Gorz, *Strategy for Labor: A Radical Proposal* (Boston, 1967).

31. Exemplary of Cole's interest in local government: "The Future of Local Government," *Political Quarterly,* 12 (1941), 405-18; "A Place Called Carradale," *New Statesman and Nation,* 18 (1939), 268-69.

32. G. D. H. Cole, *Essays in Social Theory* (London, 1950), pp. 94-95. There is, admittedly, some paternalism in this prose.

33. See Chapter 3 and the discussion of *The Meaning of Marxism* in Chapter 4.

34. Max Beloff, "G. D. H. Cole—Secular Saint?" *Encounter,* 38 (February 1972), 62-67.

35. Theodore Roszak, *The Making of a Counter-Culture* (Garden City, 1969).

36. C. Wright Mills, *White Collar* (New York, 1956); Herbert Marcuse, *One-Dimensional Man* (Boston, 1964).

37. Cole has set out and supported specific programs and policies which have been adopted—nationalization of steel, for example—but these must be considered separate and distinct from the major tenets of his philosophy, which have not been translated into policy form.

Select Bibliography

Almost any bibliography of the works of Cole, who has written thousands of books, articles, monographs, and pamphlets must necessarily be unsatisfactory. Beyond conventional sources, the reader is referred to the bibliographies in the Owen article (see below) and in Dame Margaret Cole's biography, *The Life of G. D. H. Cole.*

PRIMARY SOURCES

1. Books and Pamphlets

Attempts at General Union: A Study in British Trade Union History, 1818-1834. London: MacMillan, 1953.

The British Cooperative Movement in a Socialist Society. London: Allen and Unwin, 1951.

British Trade and Industry, Past and Future. London: Macmillan, 1932.

British Trade Unionism Today: A Survey. London: Victor Gollancz, 1939.

British Working-Class Politics, 1832-1932. London: Routledge, 1941.

Capitalism in the Modern World. London: Fabian Society, 1957.

The Case for Industrial Partnership. New York: St. Martin's Press, 1957.

A Century of Cooperation. Manchester: Allen and Unwin, 1944.

Chaos and Order in Industry. London: Methuen, 1920.

Chartist Portraits. 2nd ed. New York: St. Martin's Press, 1965.

The Development of Socialism During the Past 50 Years. London: Althone Press, 1952.

Economic Planning. 1935; rpt. Port Washington: Kennikat, 1971.

Economic Tracts for the Times. London: Macmillan, 1932.

Essays in Social Theory. London: Macmillan, 1950.

The Essentials of Socialisation. London: Fabian Research Pamphlets, 1931.

Fabian Socialism. London: Fabian Society, 1943.

The Future of Local Government. London: Cassell, 1921.

Great Britain in the Post-War World. London: Victor Gollancz, 1942.

A Guide through World Chaos. 2nd ed. New York: Knopf, 1934.

Guild Socialism Restated. London: Parsons, 1920.

A History of the Labour Party from 1914. London: Routledge, 1948.

A History of Socialist Thought. 5 vols. London: Macmillan, 1960.

The Intelligent Man's Guide through World Chaos. London: Victor Gollancz, 1932.
The Intelligent Man's Guide to the Post-War World. London: Victor Gollancz, 1947.
The Intelligent Man's Review of Europe Today. London: Victor Gollancz, 1933.
An Introduction to Trade Unionism. London: Allen and Unwin, 1953.
James Keir Hardie. London: Fabian Society, 1941.
John Burns. London: Fabian Society, 1943.
Labour's Second Term. London: Fabian Society, 1949.
The Life of Robert Owen. 3rd ed. Hamden, Connecticut: Archon, 1966.
The Life of William Cobbett. London: W. Collins, 1924.
Living Wages: The Case for a New Minimum Wage Act. London: Victor Gollancz, 1938.
Local and Regional Government. London: Cassell, 1947.
The Meaning of Marxism. London: Victor Gollancz, 1948.
The Next Ten Years in British Social and Economic Policy. London: Macmillan, 1929.
Organized Labour: An Introduction to Trade Unionism. 2nd ed., rev. London: Allen and Unwin, 1929.
Out of Work: An Introduction to the Study of Unemployment. New York: Alfred A. Knopf, 1923.
The People's Front. London: Victor Gollancz, 1937.
Persons and Periods: Studies. London: Macmillan, 1938.
A Plan for Democratic Britain. London: Labour Book Service, 1939.
Politics and Literature. New York: Harcourt, Brace, 1929.
The Post-War Condition of Britain. New York: Praeger, 1957.
Richard Carlile. London: Fabian Society, 1943.
Samuel Butler. London: Longmans, Green, 1961.
Self-Government in Industry. 1917; rpt. London: Hutchinson, 1972.
A Short History of the British Working Class Movement, 1789-1947. 3 vols. Rev. ed. London: Allen and Unwin, 1948.
The Simple Case for Socialism. London: Victor Gollancz, 1935.
Socialist Economics. London: Victor Gollancz, 1950.
Some Essentials of Socialist Propaganda. London: Fabian Society, 1932.
Some Relations Between Political and Economic Theory. London: Macmillan, 1934.
Studies in Class Structure. London: Routledge and Kegan Paul, 1955.
Studies in World Economics. 1934; rpt. Freeport: Books for Libraries, 1967.
Trade Unionism and Munitions. Oxford: Clarendon Press, 1923.
The War on the Home Front. London: Fabian Society, 1938.
What Is Wrong with the Trade Unions? London: Fabian Society, 1956.
Why Nationalise Steel? London: New Statesman Pamphlets, 1948.
William Morris as a Socialist. London: William Morris Society, 1960.

146 G. D. H. COLE

Workers' Control and Self-Government in Industry. London: Victor Gollancz, 1933.
Workshop Organisation. 1923; rpt. London: Hutchinson, 1973.
The World of Labour. 1913; rpt. New York: Barnes and Noble, 1973.
World Socialism Restated. London: New Statesman Pamphlets, 1957.
2. Collaborative Works
The Bolo Book. Ed. G. D. H. Cole and Margaret Cole. London: Labour Printing, 1921.
G. D. H. Cole and Margaret Cole. *The Condition of Britain.* London: Victor Gollancz, 1937.
G. D. H. Cole and W. Mellor. *The Meaning of Industrial Freedom.* London: Allen and Unwin, 1918.
Workers' Control and Self-Government in Industry. London: New Fabian Research Bureau, 1933.
G. D. H. Cole and Raymond Postgage. *The Common People, 1746-1946.* 4th ed. London: Methuen, 1946.
3. Articles
"The Bolshevik Revolution." *Soviet Studies,* 4 (1952), 139-51.
"The Essentials of Socialisation." *Political Quarterly,* 2 (1931), 394-410.
"The Nuffield College Social Reconstruction Survey: A Description." *Social Welfare* (of Manchester and Salford), 5 (1942), 37-42.
"Retreat from Bigness." *New Statesman and Nation,* 55 (1958), 366-67.
"Socialists and Communism." *New Statesman and Nation,* 51 (1956), 472-74.
"Thoughts After the Election." *New Statesman and Nation,* 49 (1955), 875-76.

SECONDARY SOURCES

BEER, SAMUEL H. *British Politics in the Collectivist Age.* New York: Alfred A. Knopf, 1965. The import and impact of pluralist theory as a guiding force in British politics is a theme which complements and illuminates this "mainstream" aspect of Cole's thought.
BELOFF, MAX "G. D. H. Cole—'Secular Saint'?" *Encounter, 38* (February 1972), pp. 62-67. Thoroughly interesting though nasty review of Cole's life and of Dame Margaret's biography.
Can the Workers Run Industry? Ed. Ken Coates. London: Sphere Books and Institute for Workers' Control, 1968. A thoughtful compendium for students of workers' control and Guild Socialist literature.
CARPENTER, L. P. *G. D. H. Cole: An Intellectual Biography.* Cambridge: Cambridge University Press, 1973. The only work exclusively devoted to Cole other than Dame Margaret Cole's works and the present effort. Carpenter concentrates upon Guild Socialism.
COLE, MARGARET. *Growing Up Into Revolution.* London: Longmans,

Green, 1949. A personal account of the Coles' lives which is well-written, frank, and informative.

The Life of G.D.H. Cole. New York: Macmillan, 1971. Invaluable and amazingly balanced biography in which Dame Margaret measures both accomplishments and failures but, more importantly, provides an intimate portrait and character profile.

The Story of Fabian Socialism. Stanford: Stanford University Press, 1961. Contains many good vignettes on Cole. Dame Margaret's history of the society shows that her objectivity, more often than not, overcomes her biases.

CROSLAND, C. A. R. *The Future of Socialism.* New York: Schocken, 1957. The logical end result of Collectivist thought, said Cole, is accommodation with capitalism. This book proves his point.

Essays in Labour History: In Honour of G. D. H. Cole. Ed. Asa Briggs and John Saville. London: Macmillan, 1960. The reminiscences on Cole at different points in his life, which appear in the introductory section, are the principal value of this work.

FREMANTLE, ANNE. *This Little Band of Prophets: The British Fabians.* New York: New American Library, 1960. An inaccurate and unreliable guide on both Fabians and Fabianism, including Cole.

GLASS, S.T. *The Responsible Society: The Ideas of the English Guild Socialists.* London: Longmans, Green, 1966. The best introduction available to the rudiments and origins of Guild Socialist thought.

The Incompatibles: Trade Union Militancy and the Consensus. Ed. Robin Blackburn and Alexander Cockburn. Harmondsworth: Penguin, 1967. Sponsored by the Neo-Marxist *New Left Review,* the majority of these readings are updated treatments of concerns of Cole.

Industrial Democracy in Great Britain: A Book of Readings and Witnesses for Workers' Control. Ed. Ken Coates and Tony Topham. London: Macgibbon and Kee, 1968. A more recent expression of Cole's concerns, but it includes an excerpt from a source as old as his 1920 *Guild Socialism Restated.*

JENKINS, DAVID *Job Power: Blue and White Collar Democracy.* Baltimore: Penguin, 1973. Innovative and valuable interdisciplinary focus on the subject by an inheritor of Guild Socialist traditions and concerns.

MARTIN, KINGSLEY, *Editor.* London: Hutchinson, 1968. Autobiographical work of Cole's close *New Statesman* compatriot.

"G. D. H. Cole." *New Statesman and Nation,* 57 (1959), 63. Obituary written by a fond friend which summarizes Cole's accomplishments and character.

MILIBAND, RALPH. *Parliamentary Socialism.* London: Allen and Unwin, 1961. Miliband is a Marxist, but his views on the Labour party, "the sickness of Labourism," and the impossibility of evolutionary

Socialism strike several chords that are resonant in Cole.

MORRIS, WILLIAM. *News from Nowhere.* 1891; rpt. London: Routledge, 1970. The primary influence upon Cole's thought.

OWEN, GAIL L. "G. D. H. Cole's Historical Writings." *International Review of Social History*, 2 (1966), 169-96. Excellent bibliographical piece which helps researchers through a particularly dense thicket of Cole's work.

PEASE, EDWARD R. *The History of the Fabian Society.* London: Methuen, 1946. History of the society from the standpoint of its first and very faithful secretary. Introduction by Margaret Cole.

ROUSSEAU, JEAN-JACQUES. *The Social Contract and Discourses.* Ed. G. D. H. Cole. New York: E. P. Dutton, 1932. Cole's lengthy introduction provides special insights on Rousseau, though very little can be discerned of Cole by reading it.

SOREL, GEORGES. *Reflections on Violence.* Glencoe: Free Press, 1950. The "bible" of Syndicalists, from whom Guild Socialists gathered some of their roots.

TAYLOR, A. J. P. "A Bolshevik Soul in a Fabian Muzzle." *New Statesman,* 82 (1971), 441-42. Taylor "venerated" Cole, and this is obvious in his review of Dame Margaret's biography.

ULAM, ADAM. *The Philosophical Origins of British Socialism.* Cambridge: Harvard University Press, 1951. Explains how Cole might have been influenced and also helps to explain forces with which Cole had to contend.

WEBB, BEATRICE. *Diaries 1912-24* and *Diaries 1924-32.* Ed. Margaret Cole. A rich trove of Fabian activities and figures from a personal viewpoint.

The Webbs and Their Work. Ed. Margaret Cole. Hassocks near Brighton: Harvester Press, 1976 (new edition). Vital for an understanding of the love-hate relationship of the Coles and the Webbs.

Index

149

Syndicalism, 29, 30, 36, 50, 53, 54, 58, 77, 103

Tanzania, 89
Tawney, R.H., 52, 109
Taylor, A.J.P., 22
Technology, 43, 47, 51, 57, 74, 75, 81, 87, 110, 111, 122-24, 125
Tito, Josep Broz, 40, 106, 115
Titoists, 89
Tories, 14, 36, 37, 40, 44, 49, 60, 74, 75, 112; See also—Conservative party
Trade unions, 14, 15, 18-19, 20, 24, 25, 41, 43, 53, 54, 68, 73, 74, 75, 78, 80, 105, 108, 115; bureaucratization of, 19, 68, 75, 125; craft unions, 79; in America, 19, 43, 101, 105; industrial unionism, 79-80; structure, 19
Trades Union Congress (TUC), 43, 116
Transport and General Workers Union (TGWU), 116
Trotsky, Leon, 104, 105
Trotskyists, 93, 104, 105
Truman, Harry S., 40

Union of Soviet Socialists Republics (U.S.S.R.), (Soviet Union), 13, 17, 30, 31, 36, 39, 40, 70, 92
Unionism—see trade unions
United Nations, 120

United States of America, 13, 19, 25, 26, 29, 39, 40, 41, 43, 54, 55, 70, 74, 79, 101, 105, 116, 120, 121, 125
University College, 33
Utopian Socialism, 49, 51, 61, 69, 78, 82, 88, 90, 91, 112

Vienna Union, 105
Von Mises, Ludwig, 63-64, 110

Wales, 35
Wallas, Graham, 16
Webb, Beatrice, 16-17, 23, 29, 30, 31, 41, 53, 66, 75, 109, 112
Webb, Sydney, 16-17, 29, 30, 31, 41, 53, 66, 75, 109, 112
Weber, Max, 96
Wells, H.G., 16, 47
Welwyn Garden City, 32
West Germany, 70
Workers Educational Association, 20, 24-25, 34, 43
Working conditions, 48-49, 74, 81, 85, 87, 88, 116-19, 125; under nationalization, 68
World Socialist Crusade, 69, 70
World War I, 73, 100, 104
World War II, 13, 37-39, 41, 87, 97, 105

Yugoslavia, 40, 74, 89, 106, 114, 115, 116, 117